Photographs by Michael Cinquino
Book design by Vanessa Paolantonio

Published by cnq photography, llc.
Brooklyn, NY

www.michaelcinquino.com

ISBN 978-0-9857-5751-9

Printed in the United States of America

Naked Girls on
POLAROID

MICHAEL CINQUINO

Thank you to the twenty-five
brave and beautiful women who
made this book possible.
And, to the one who I couldn't do it without.

Sadly, **film may soon be a thing of the past**. With the recent Kodak bankruptcy and very few other film manufacturers left standing, the odds that you'll even be able to get a roll of film in the next five to ten years isn't good at all. Pro labs that develop film are fewer and fewer as well. And my camera of choice, Nikon, only manufactures two film models in it's entire thirty-nine camera line up. Soon those may disappear as well.

I began my career as a digital photographer. I knew nothing about film photography when I first picked up a camera. After about two years of shooting digital, I met a photographer whose work I admired very much: Dean Lavery. Dean told me that if I really wanted to be a *great* photographer, I had to shoot medium format film. I asked him 'why?' he said: "just do it and let me know if you have questions." That same day I bought a used Bronica ETRS 120 film camera. He was right. With only sixteen exposures on a roll of film I really had to slow down and give great care to each click of the shutter (I was used to shooting hundred of frames in a single session on digital) and, in just a matter of weeks, my skill as both a film and digital photographer had improved greatly. There was something else I noticed. . . .

There was a humanness that my subjects had on film that they lacked in digital photos. It's hard to put into words but the best way I can describe it is that people looked more like people and less like images. I know there are a bunch of technical (and chemical) reasons behind this but since my focus tends more towards results and less towards process, the details weren't nearly as important as what I saw when I looked at both side by side.

Soon after I began as a film photographer, I had the privilege of assisting a photographer named George Pitts on a shoot. George only shoots film. On every shoot he has two cameras, a Mamiya C330 120 film camera and a Polaroid 600SE instant camera. I'd never seen a 600SE until that day. What it looks like is here:

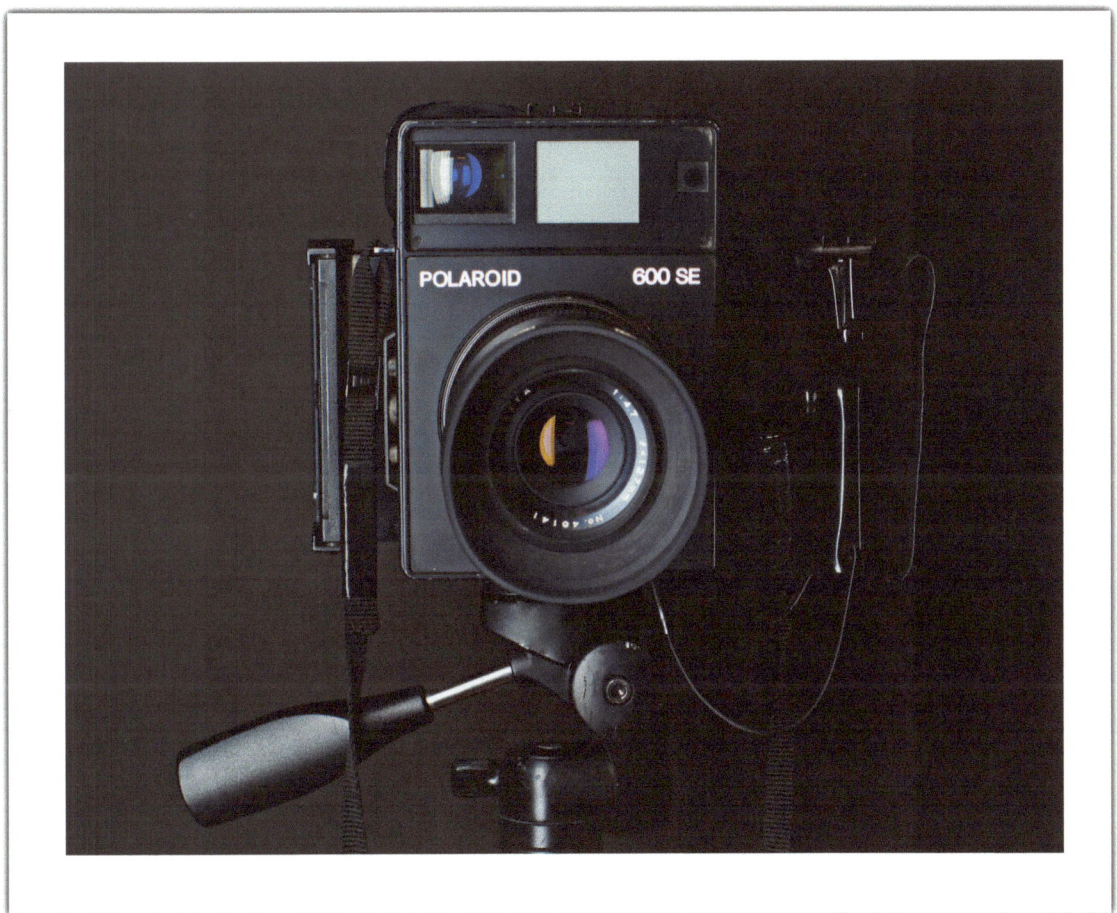

When I saw the quality of the photos that were coming out of George's 600SE I was instantly in love (pun intended) and knew I had to have one, two months later I did. I've been shooting on it for over a year now and it's my favorite camera by far, of the seven others I own.

My idea for this book came as a result of a few bits of inspiration. I mentioned earlier that I began my career as a digital photographer. This is true. What is also true of when I first began is that most of what I shot were nudes. And, more directly, what started as a great excuse to get girls naked in my Hell's Kitchen apartment turned into a genuine love (and obsession) of photography. I was shooting on, essentially, a one-megapixel point and shoot and had absolutely no idea what I was doing photographically. What I did know, however, is that if I wanted to *keep* shooting naked girls I had to make them feel comfortable and look absolutely beautiful. I did both very well. Word got out and I soon had a bunch of girls wanting me to shoot them nude. Nope, that didn't suck.

I got better each time I shot. Eventually, I took what I had learned and applied it to headshots and portraiture and soon found myself with a blossoming career. I have since moved on from nude work and don't shoot much of it anymore. This book, however, has helped me honor where I began.

It is also a tribute to the medium of film; *Instant* film to be exact and, particularly, its simplicity and authenticity. In using the Polaroid 600SE camera for this project all I needed was film, some light, and a model and I was able to create something. I didn't even need electricity (but I did use some).

Lastly, in our digital age, I believe us human beings yearn for authenticity—things that are genuine, simple, and pure. Ironically, some of that authenticity, for me, came from a cutting edge technology introduced on February 21, 1947 when Edwin H. Land unveiled his instant camera and associated film: the "Land Camera." Sixty-five years have passed since the invention of that camera and it's still relevant today. Just ask those Instagram guys who sold their company for a billion dollars—never would have happed if it wasn't for Dr. Land.

For me, it doesn't get more authentic than nude portraits on instant film. Which is what you'll find in the pages of this book: Over one hundred photos of twenty-five New York City women photographed exclusively on instant film. The majority of these women have never modeled before, let alone nude. They are women from all walks of life: a yoga teacher, an office manager, a musician, an advertising manager ranging in age from twenty-two to forty-one. I would call them normal, everyday girls but they're not. They are extraordinary, unique, and beautiful women who all dove in to create something authentic and meaningful. I'm honored to have worked with each and every one of them and may this book be something they're proud to show their grandkids!

I must, of course, thank you, the reader/viewer, for picking up my book. That you are reading these words right now excites me to no end. And I believe you'll find both beauty and authenticity in this book just as I have in it's creation.

With Gratitude,

Michael Cinquino
Photographer

And if a day goes by without my doing some-thing related to photography, it's as though I've neglected something essential to my existence, as though I had forgotten to wake up. I know that the accident of my being a photographer has made my life possible.

—Richard Avedon

Tanya

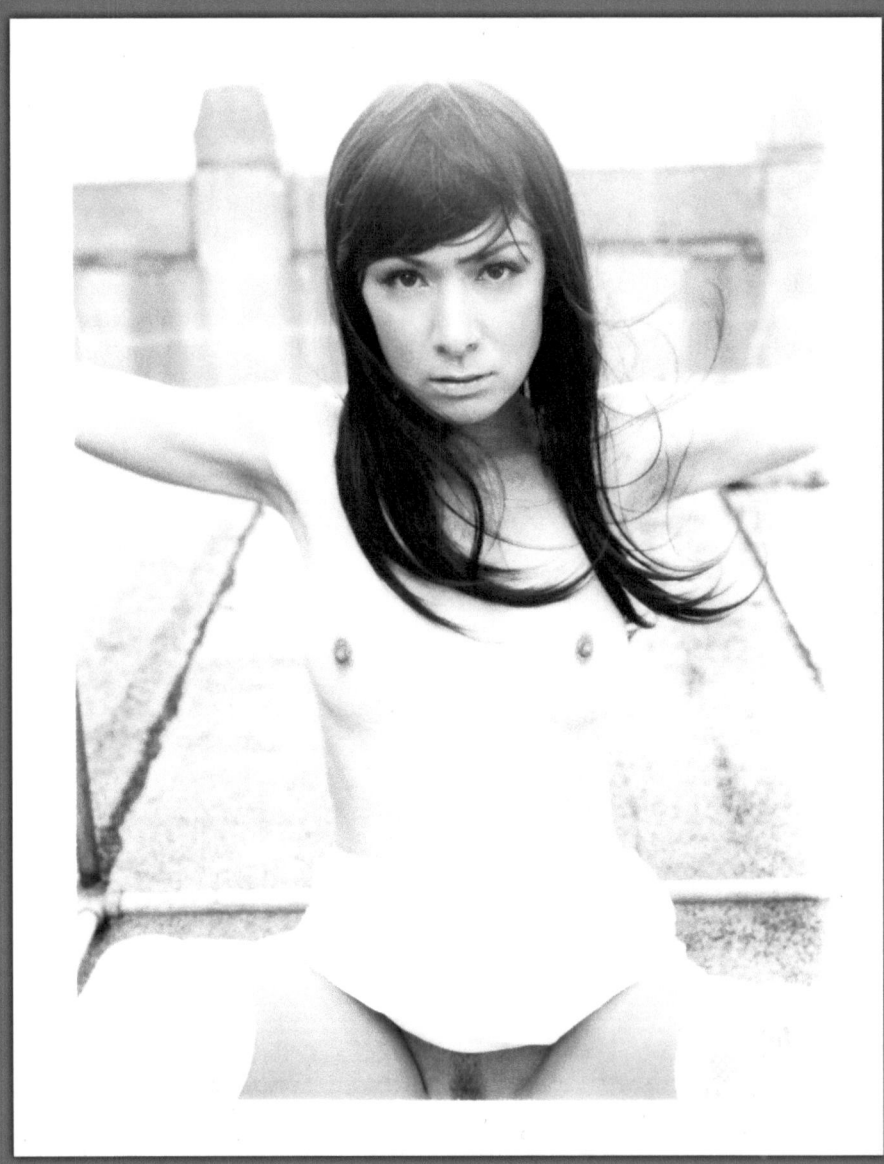

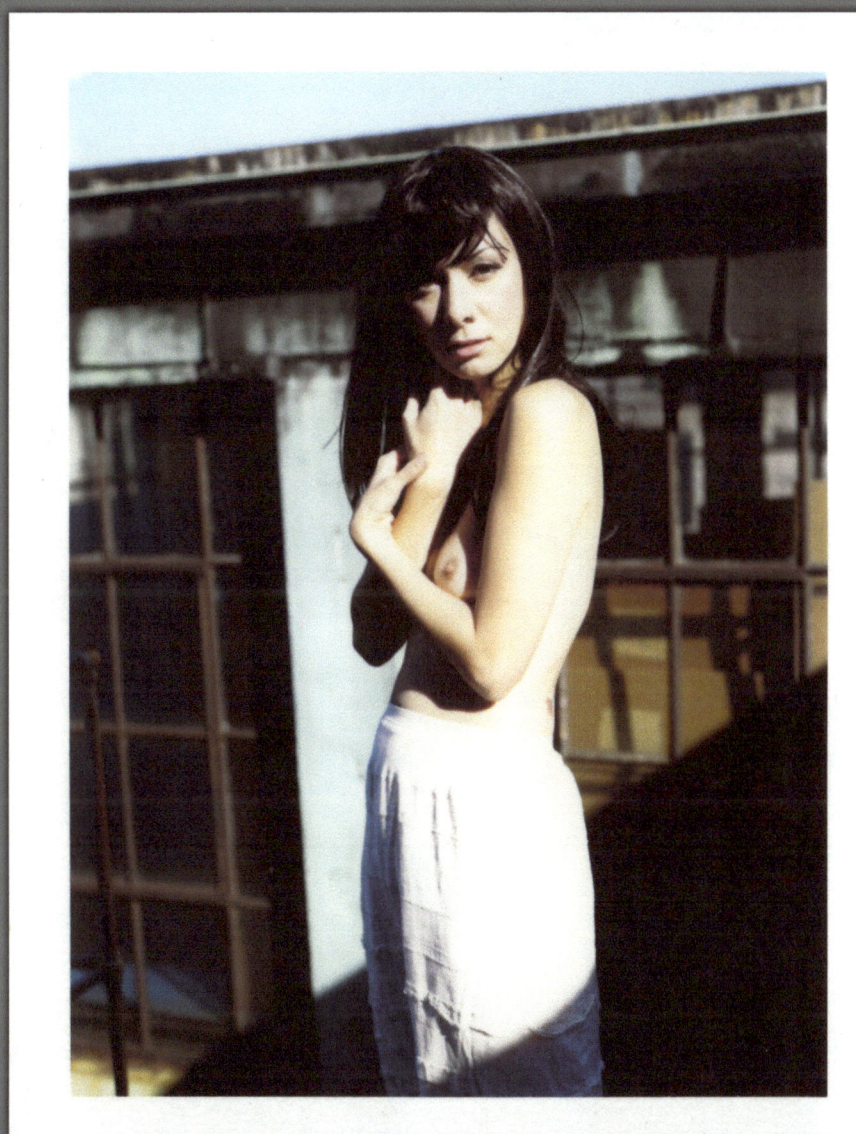

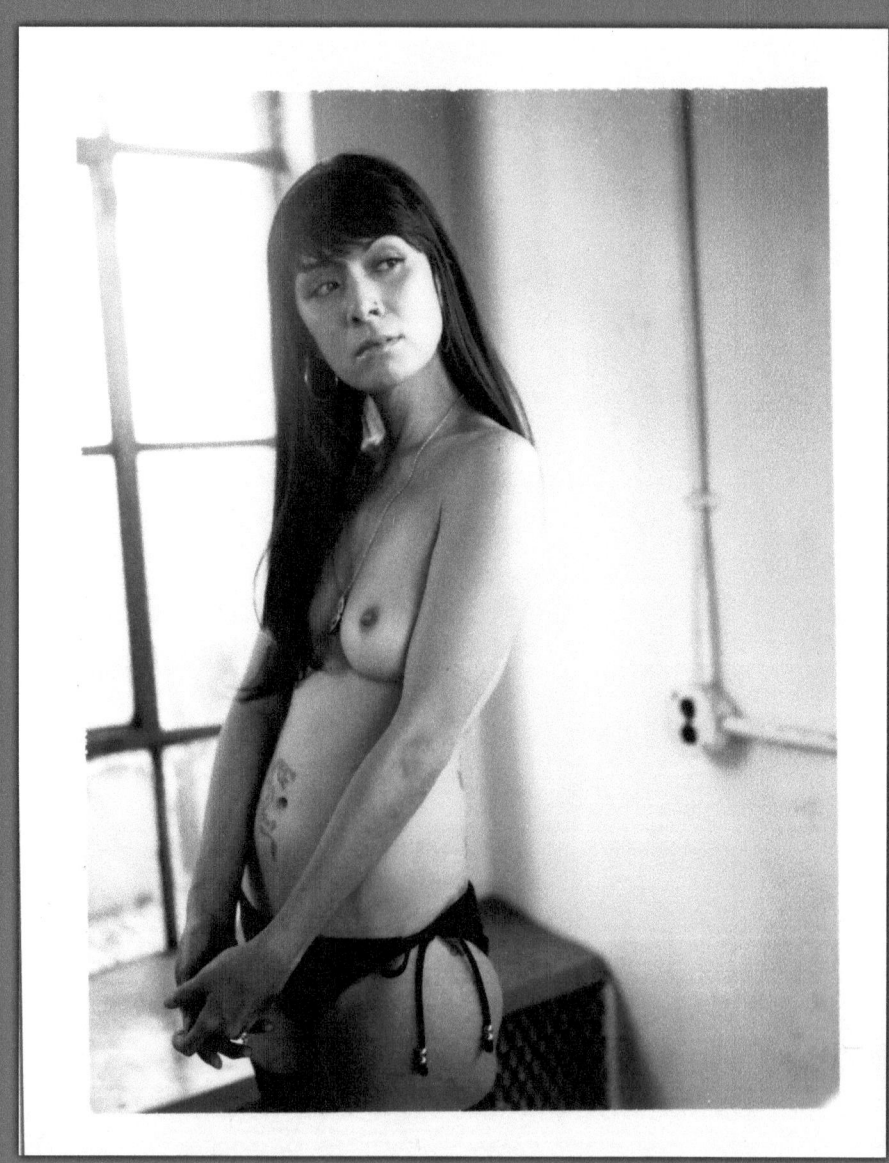

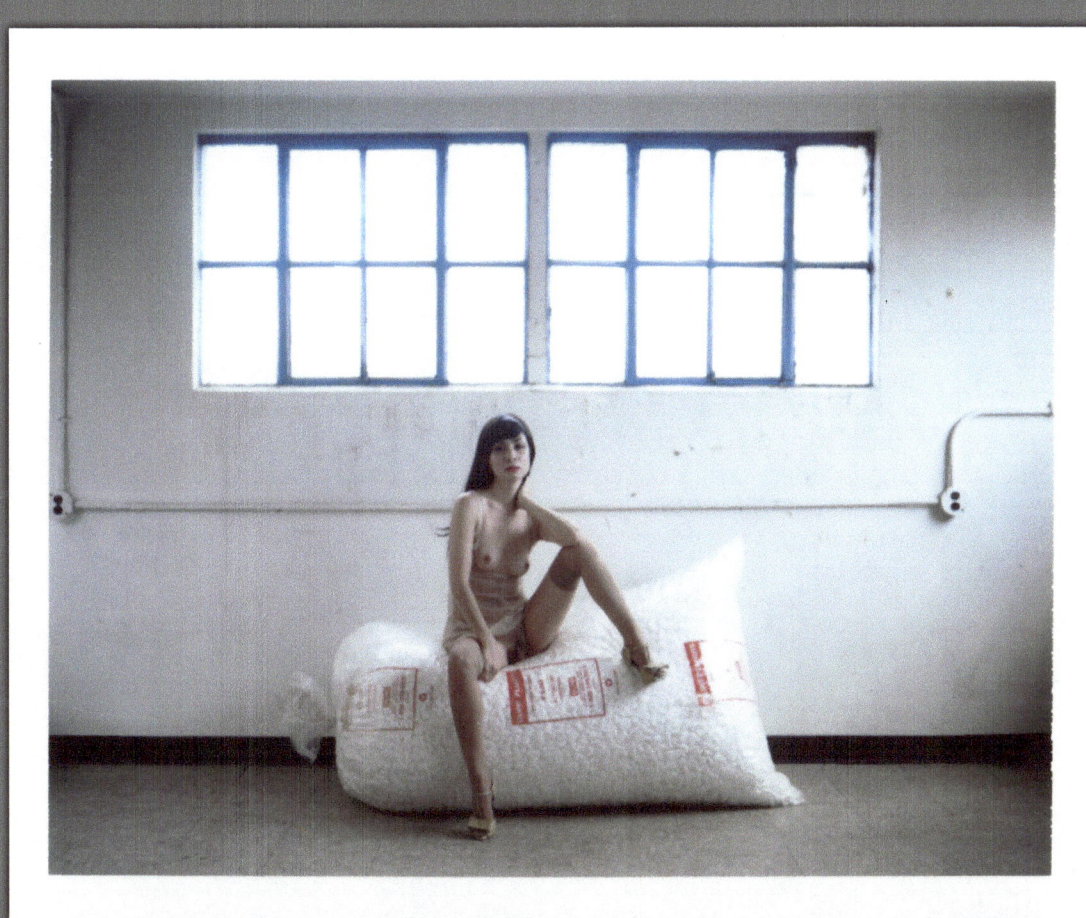

Sophie

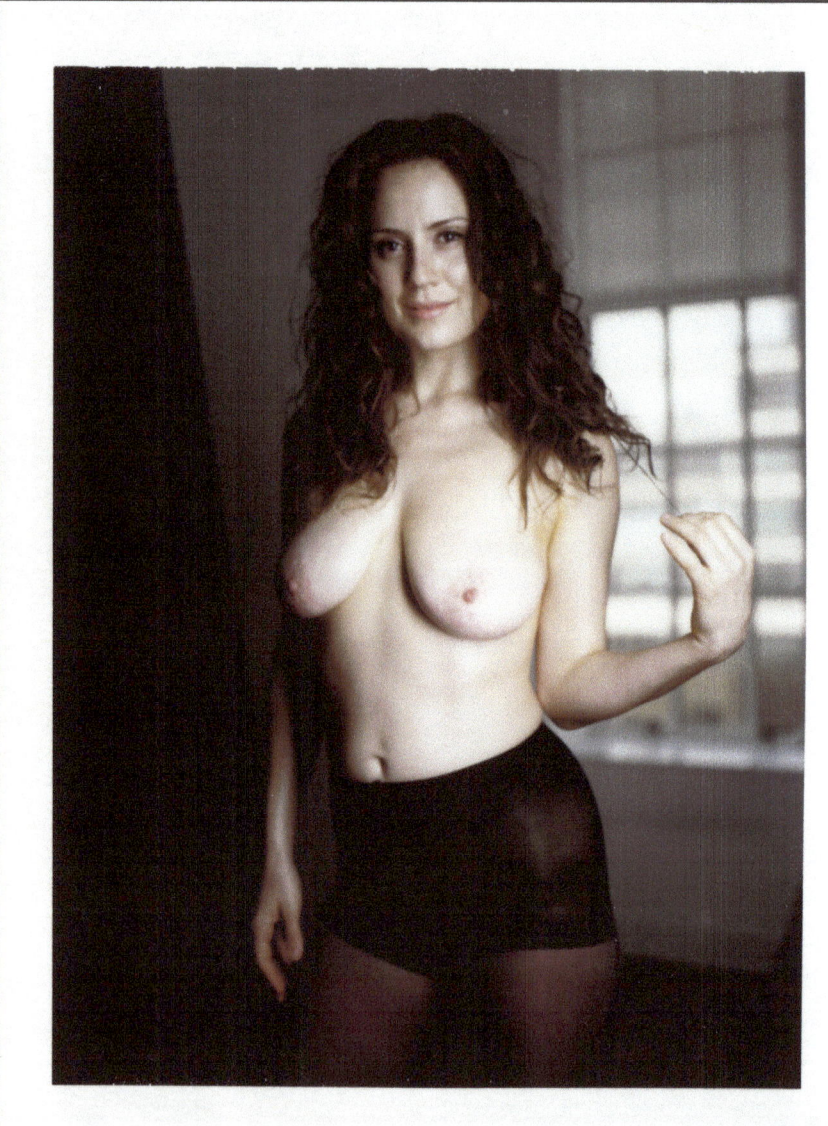

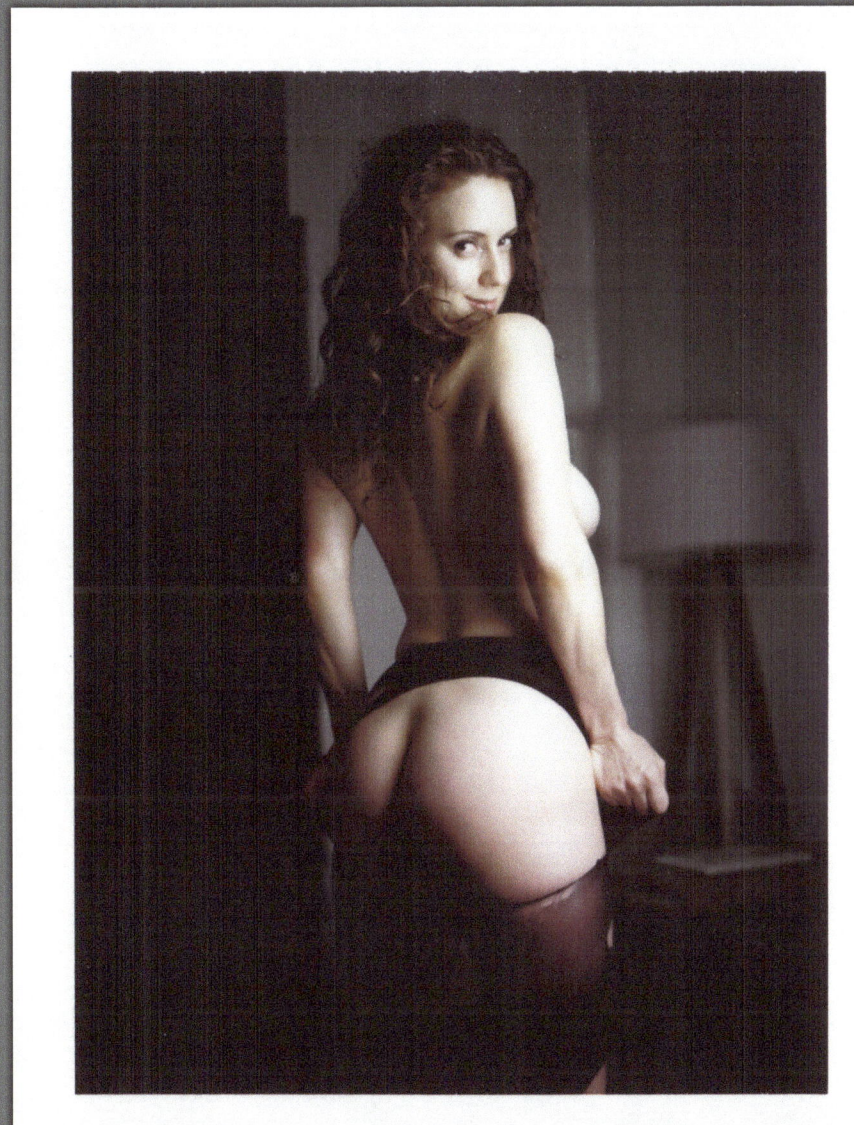

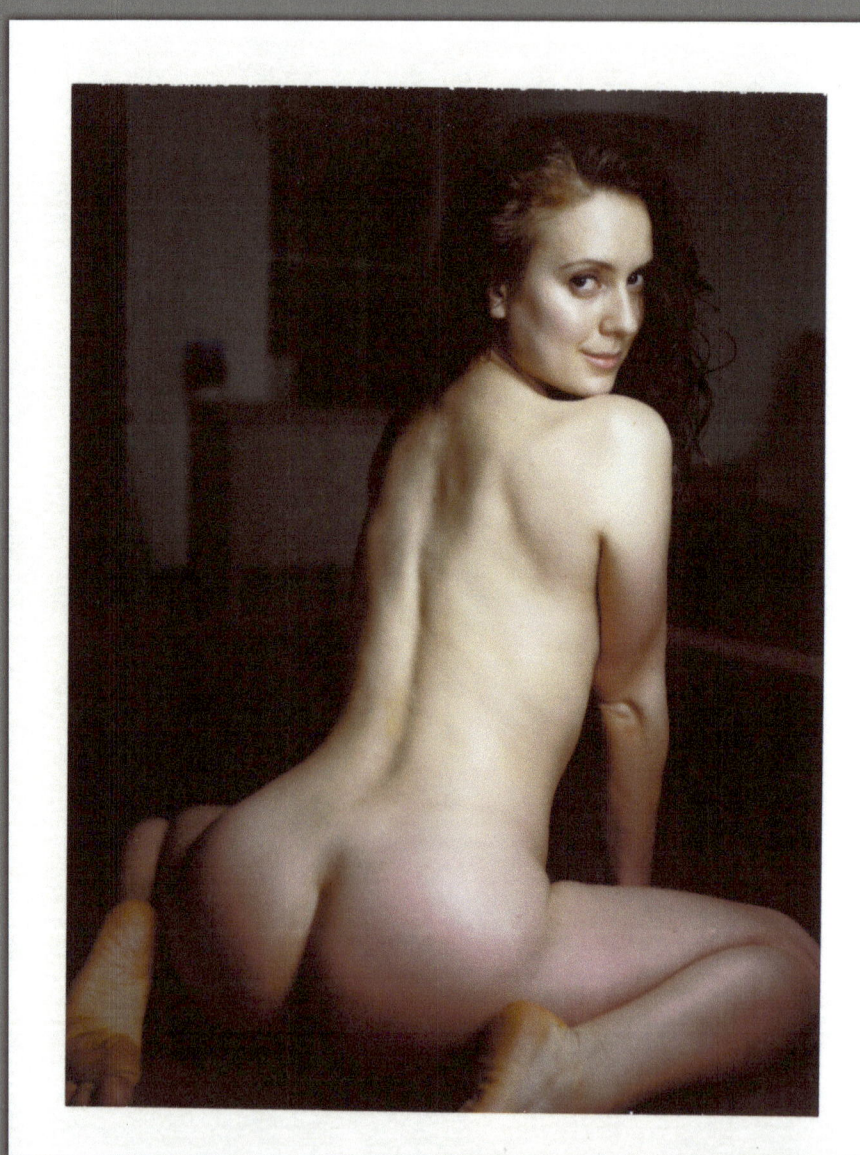

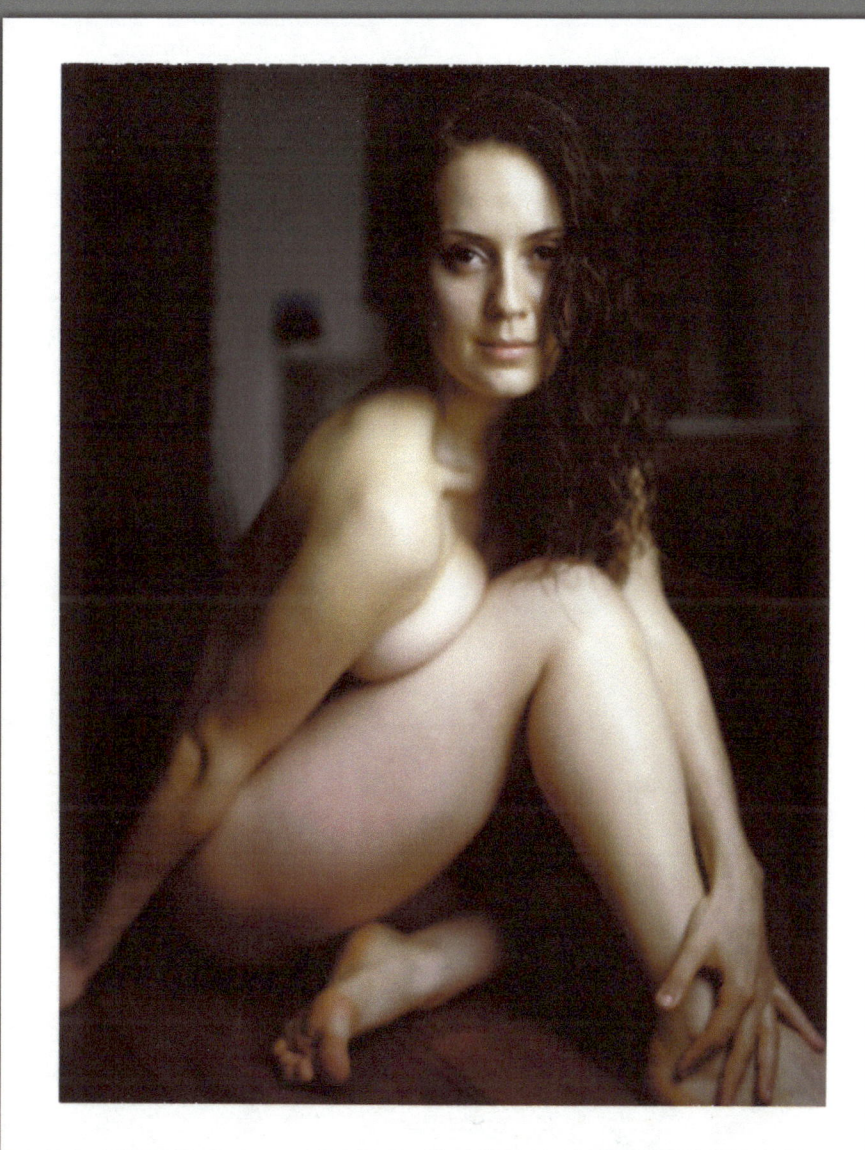

April

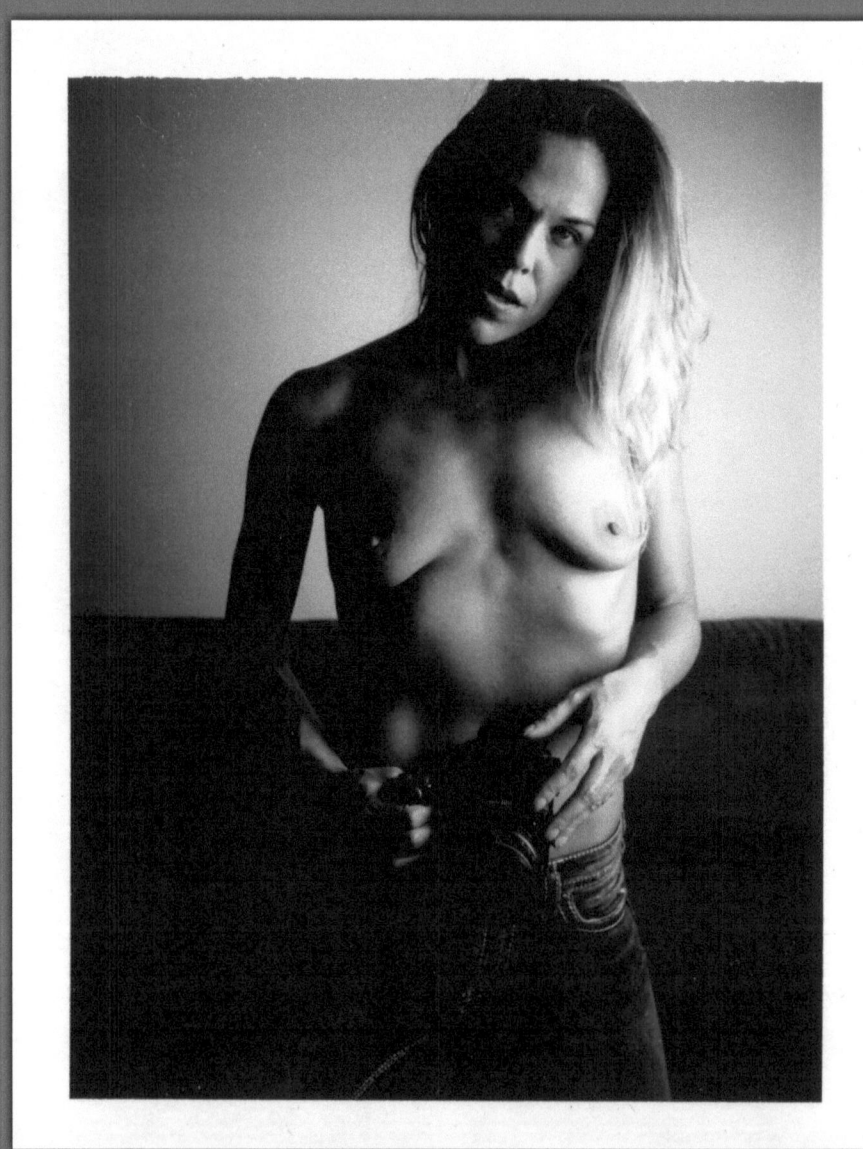

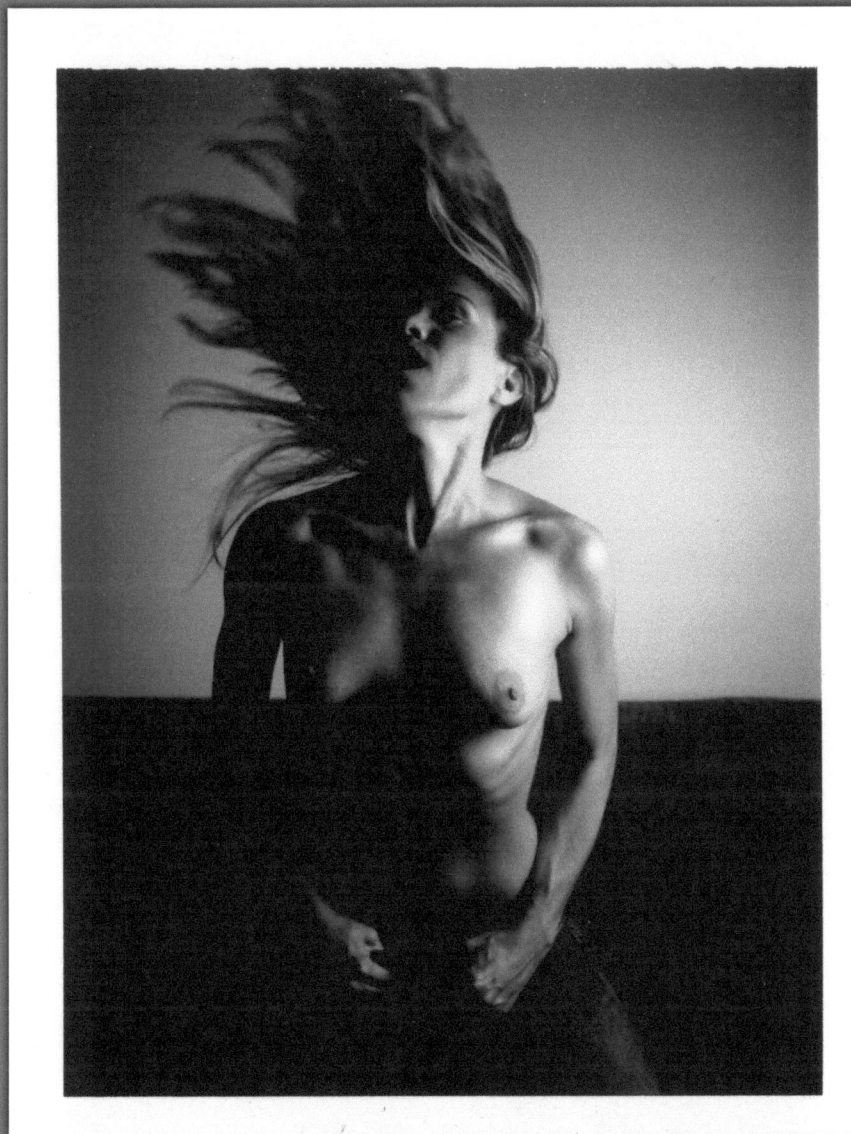

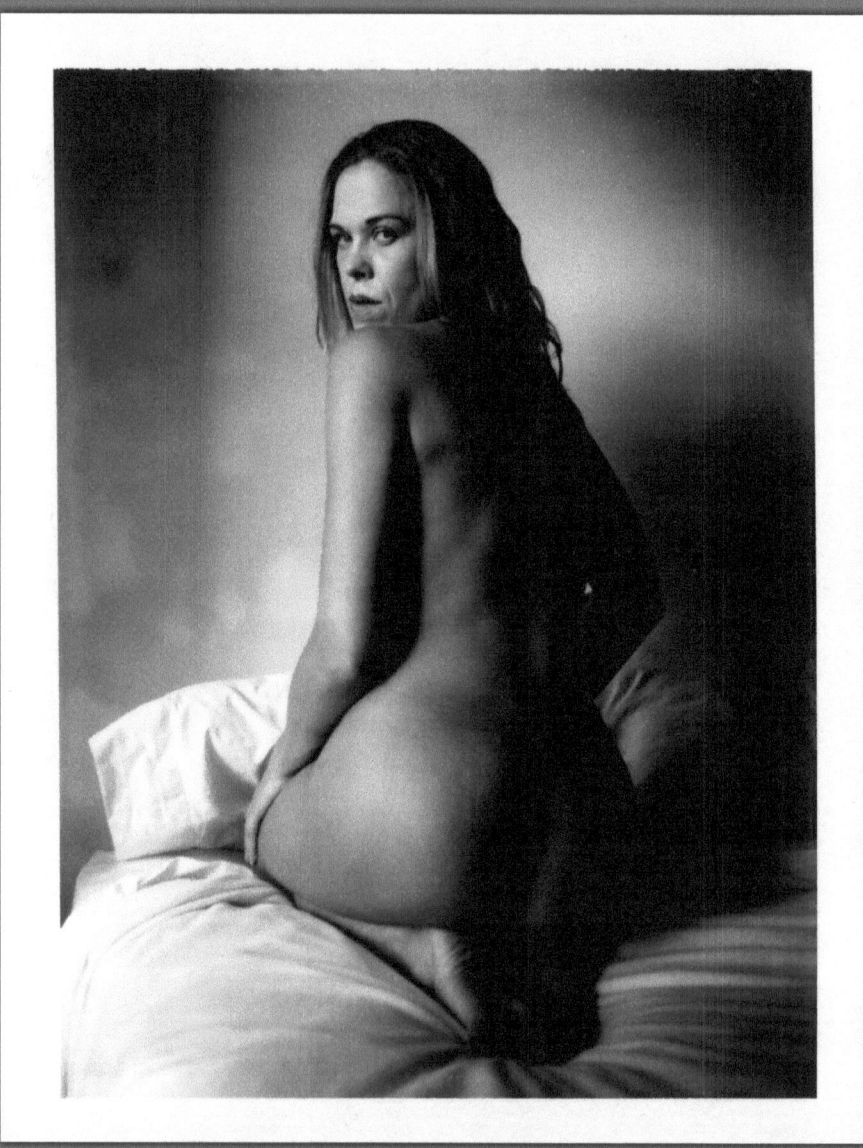

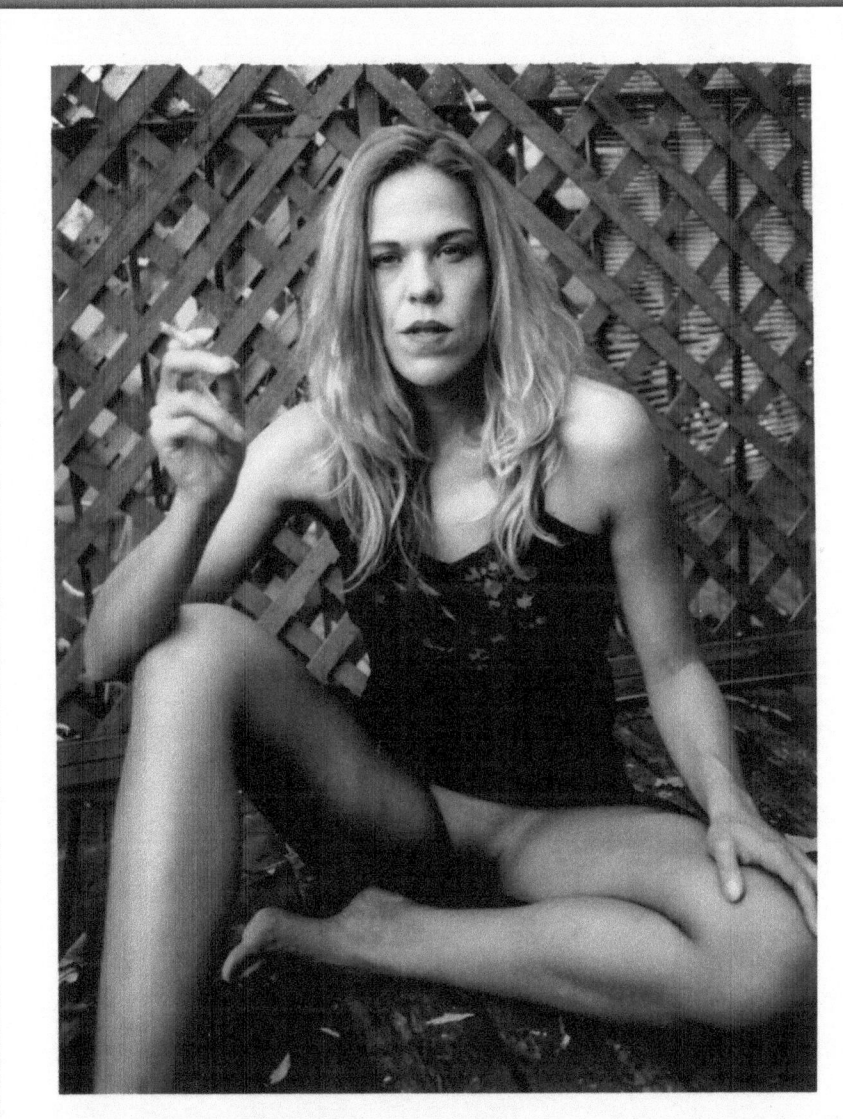

Rachel

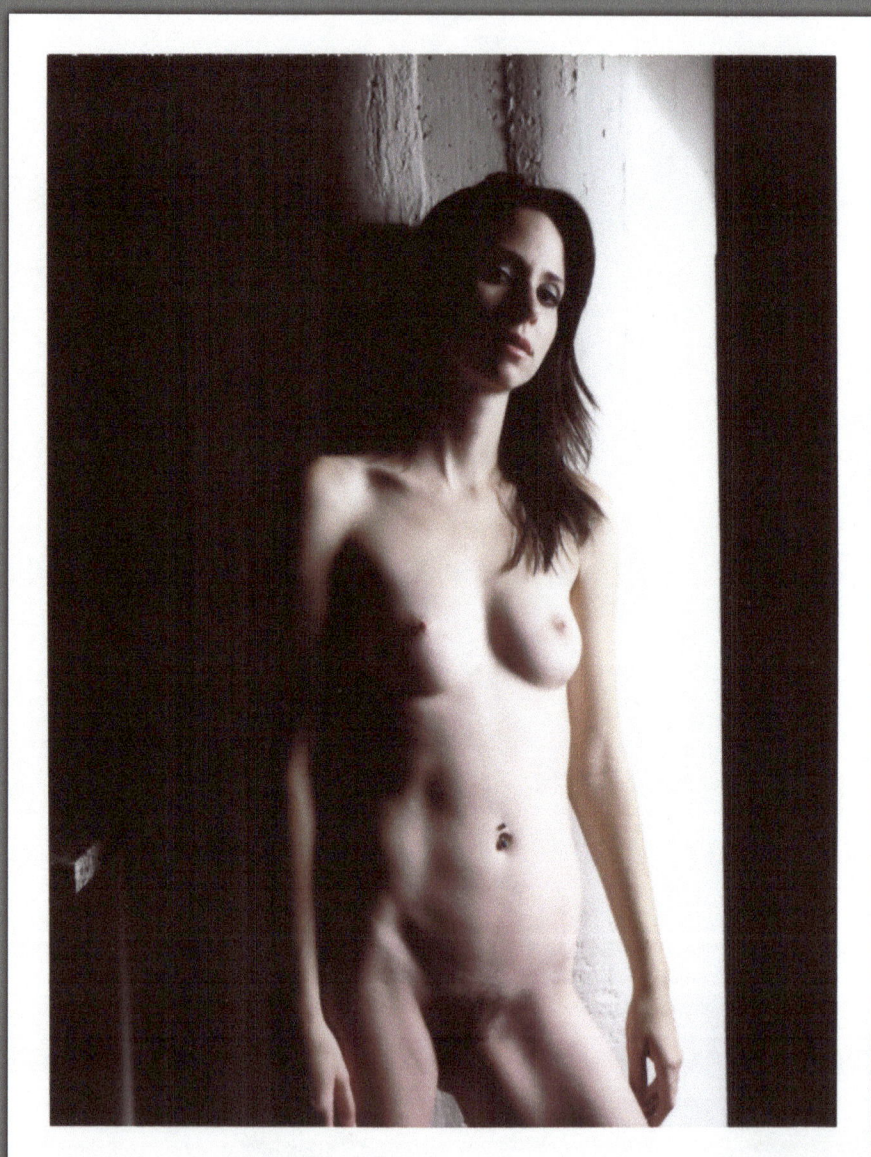

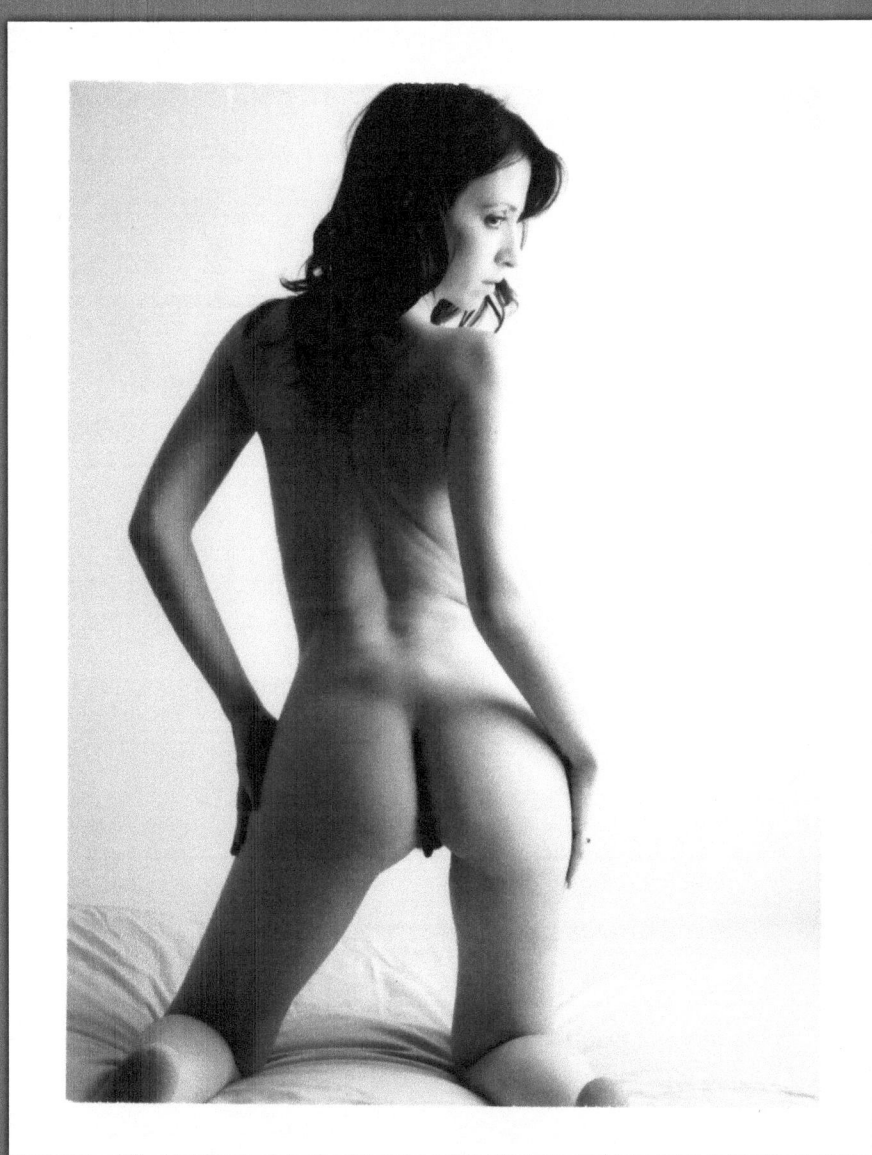

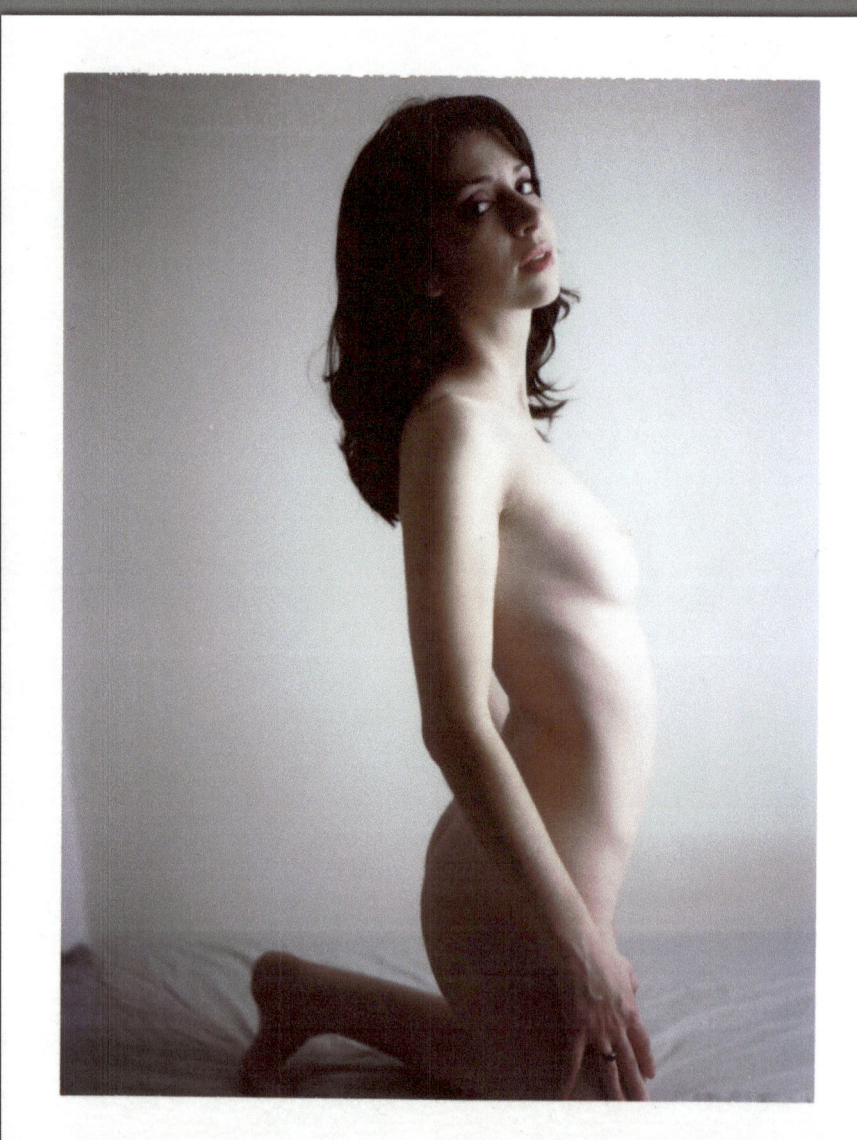

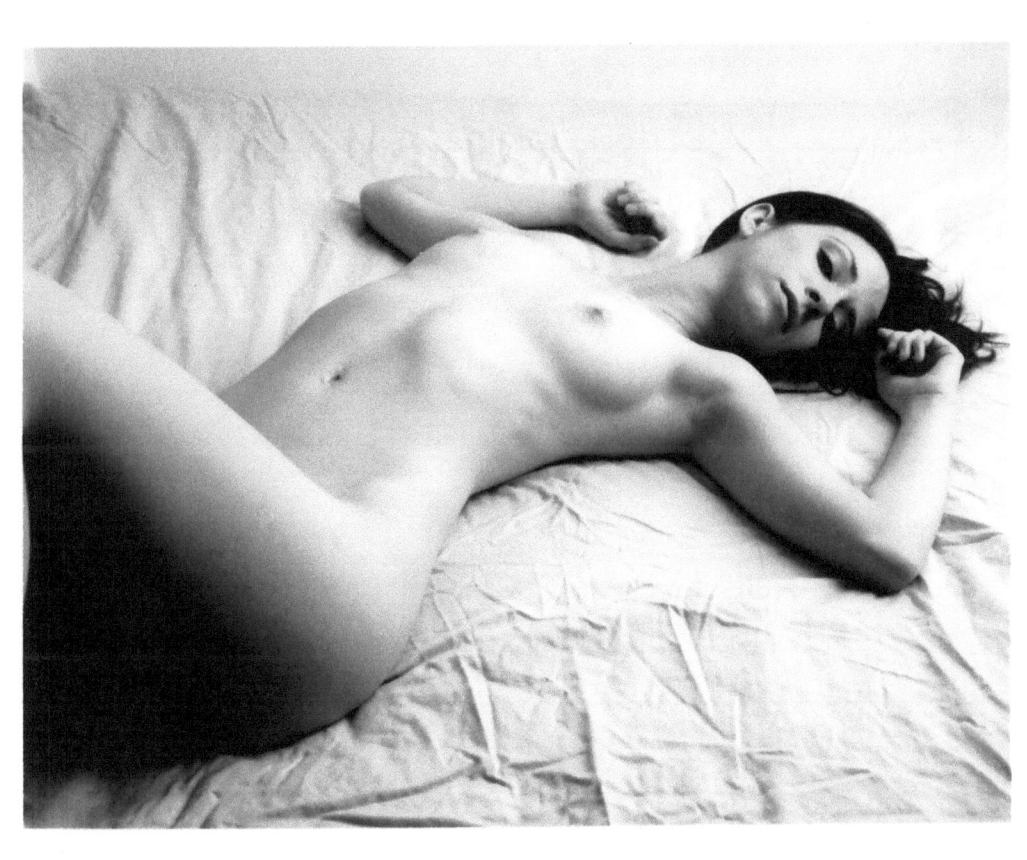

Raquel

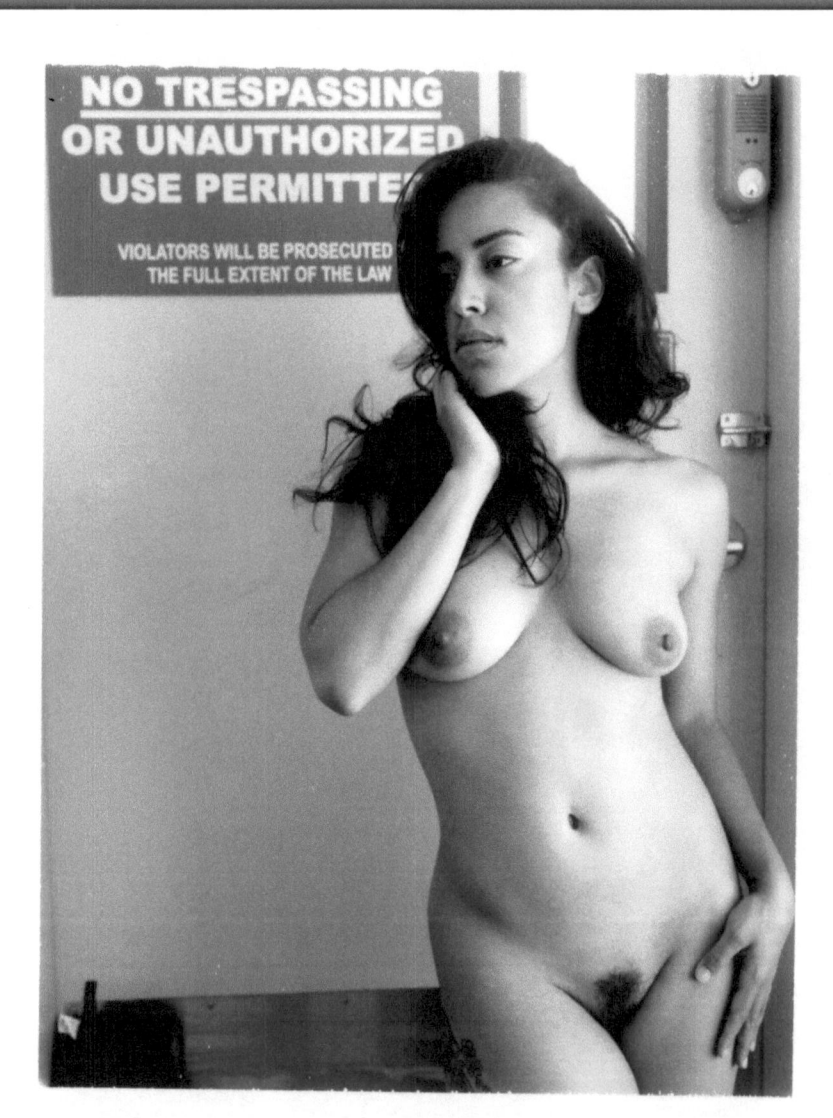

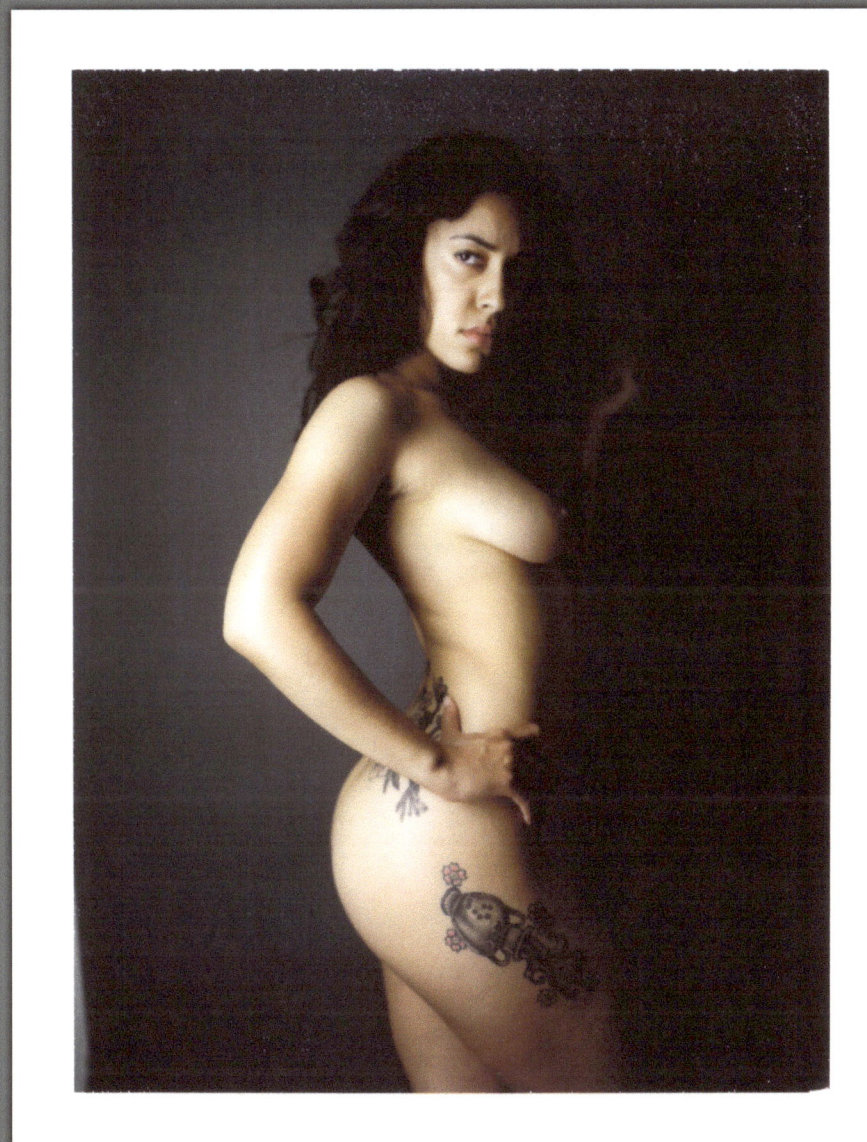

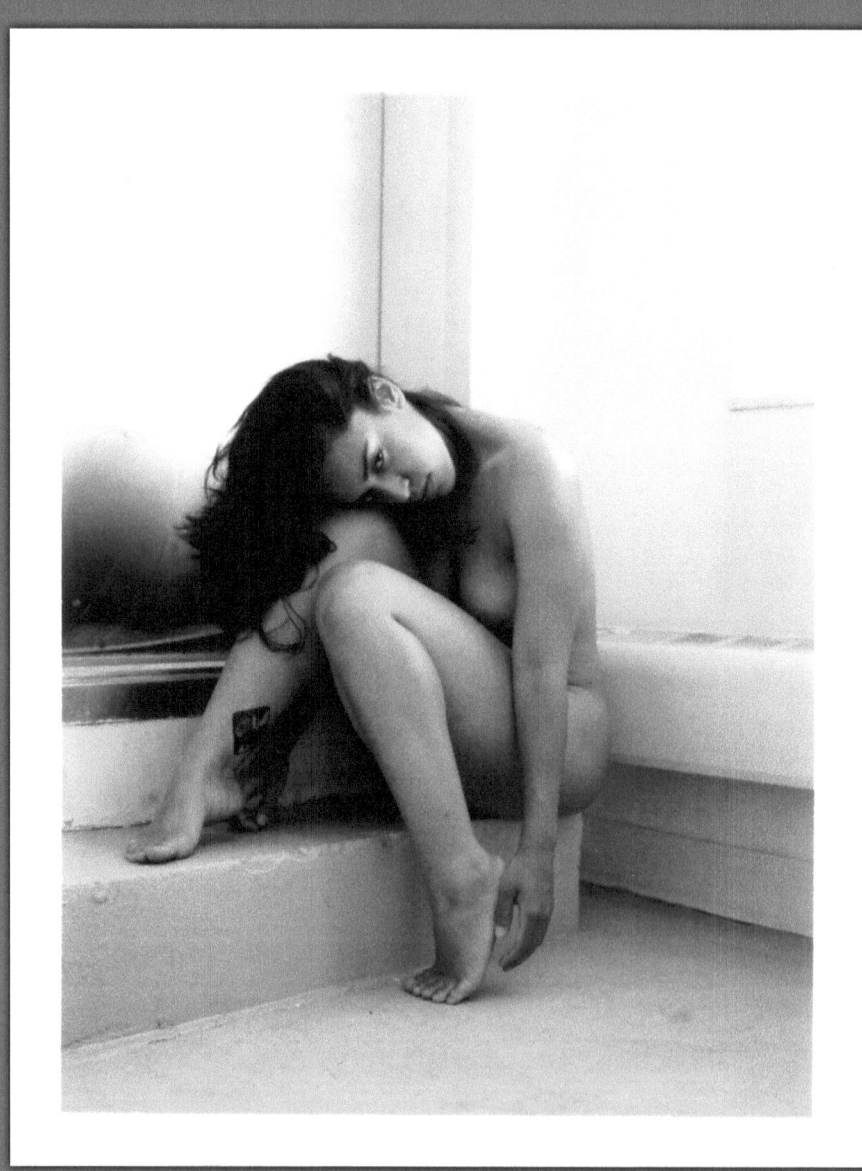

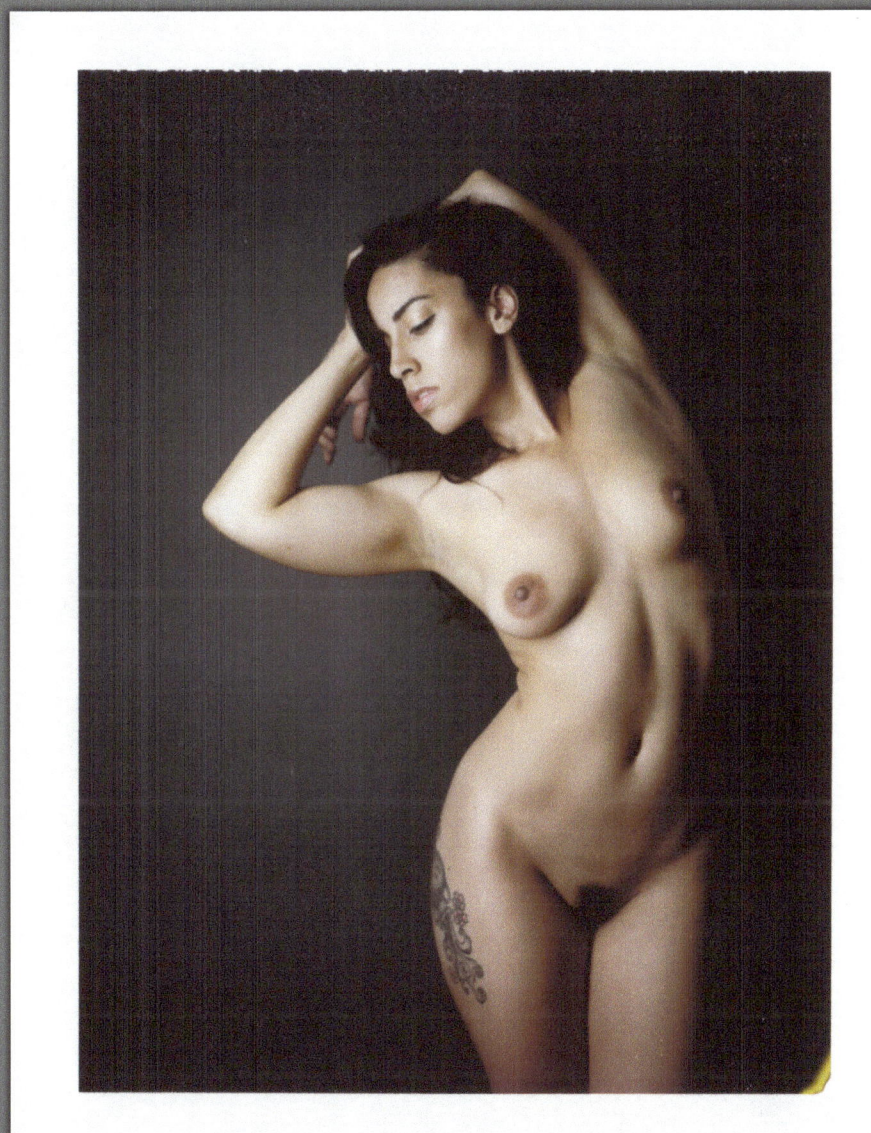

Amanda

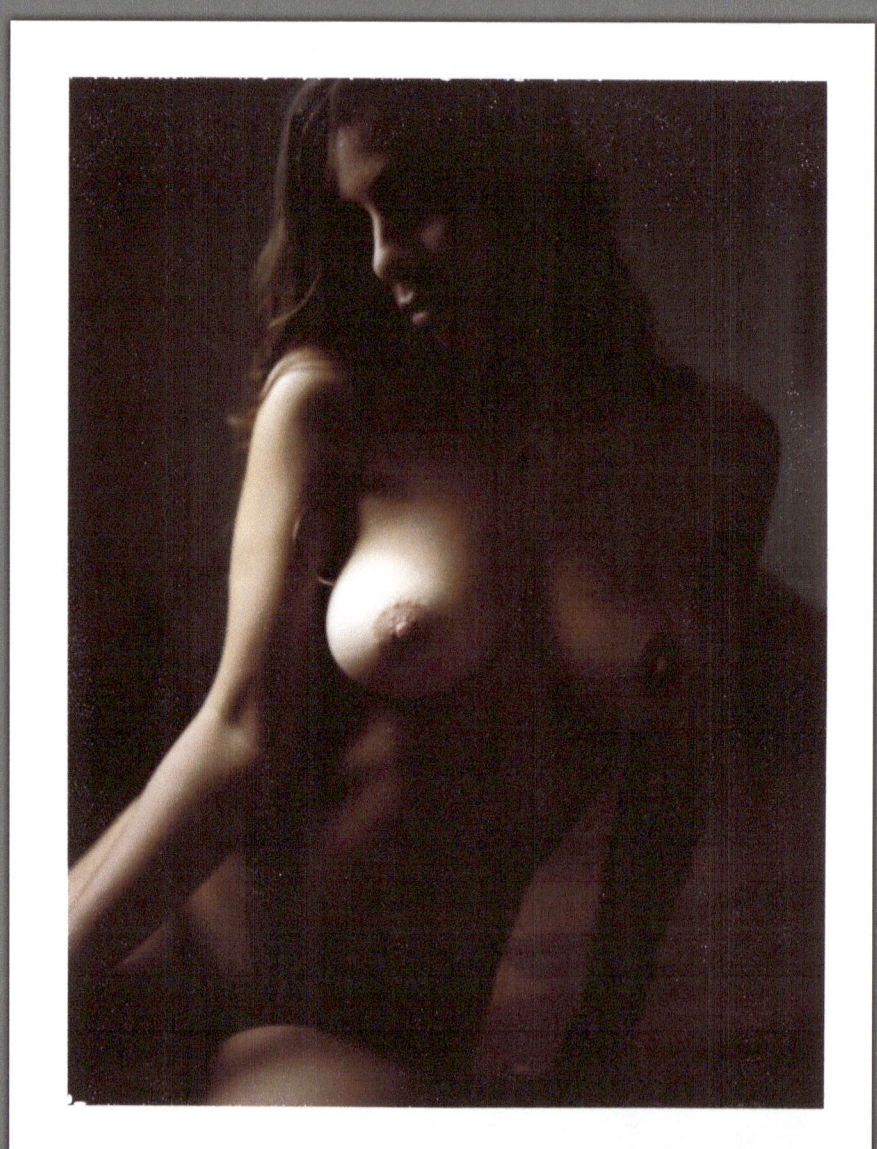

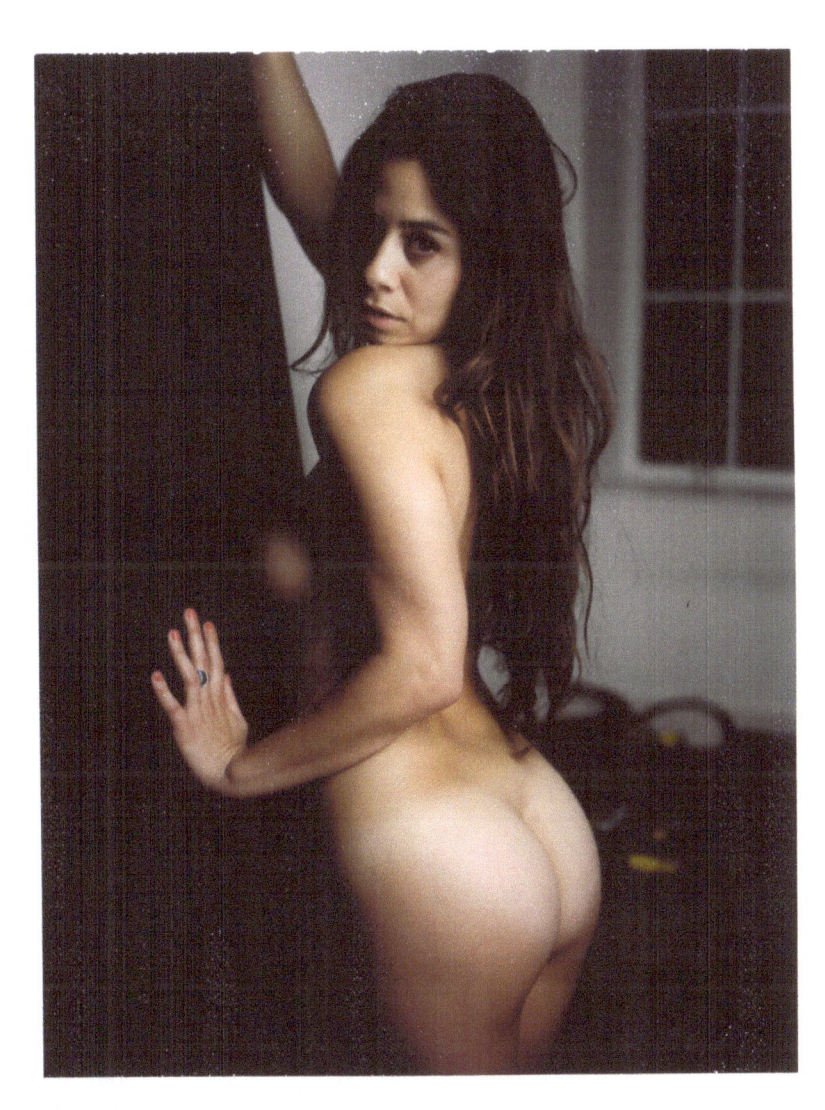

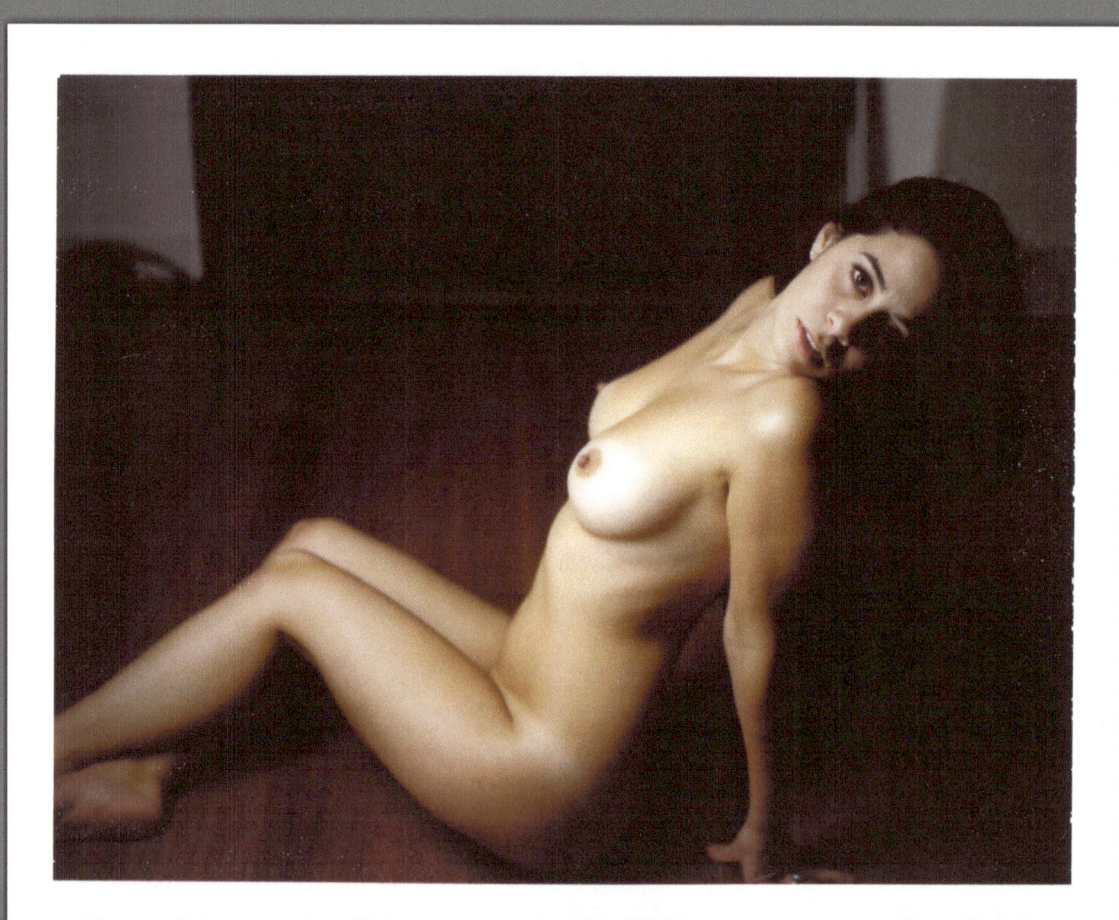

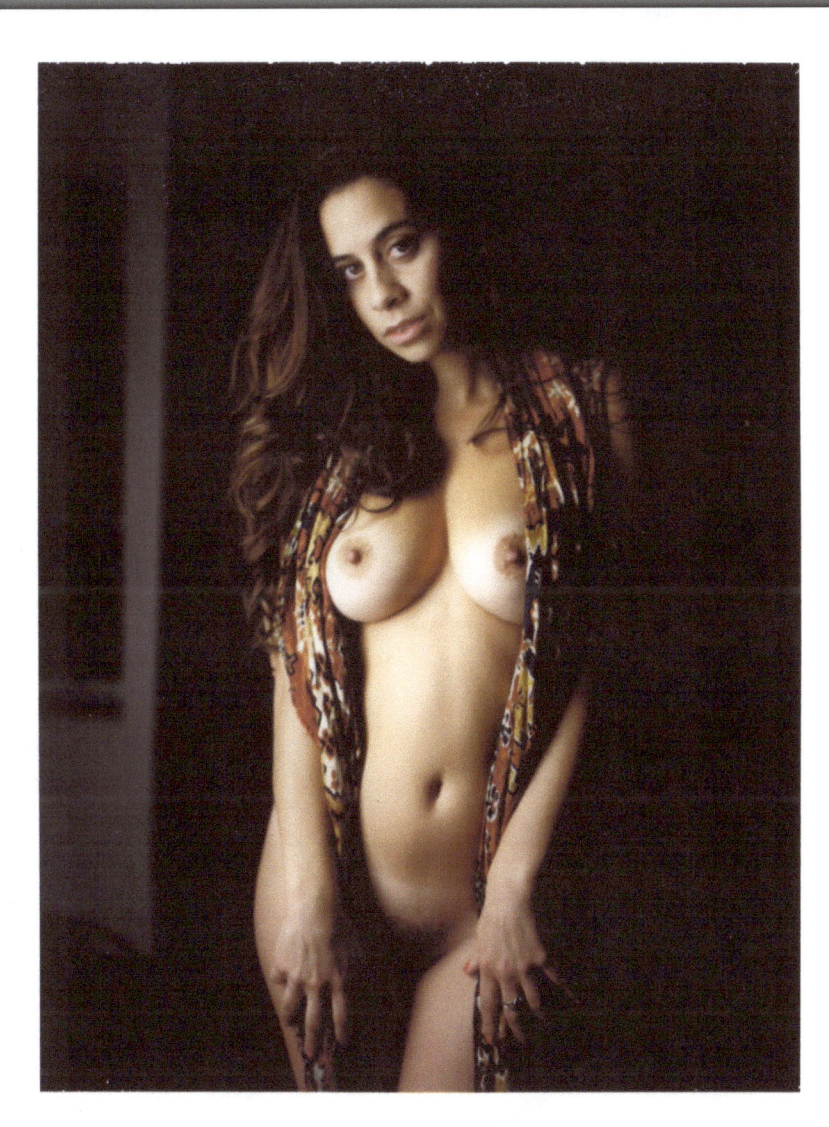

Megan

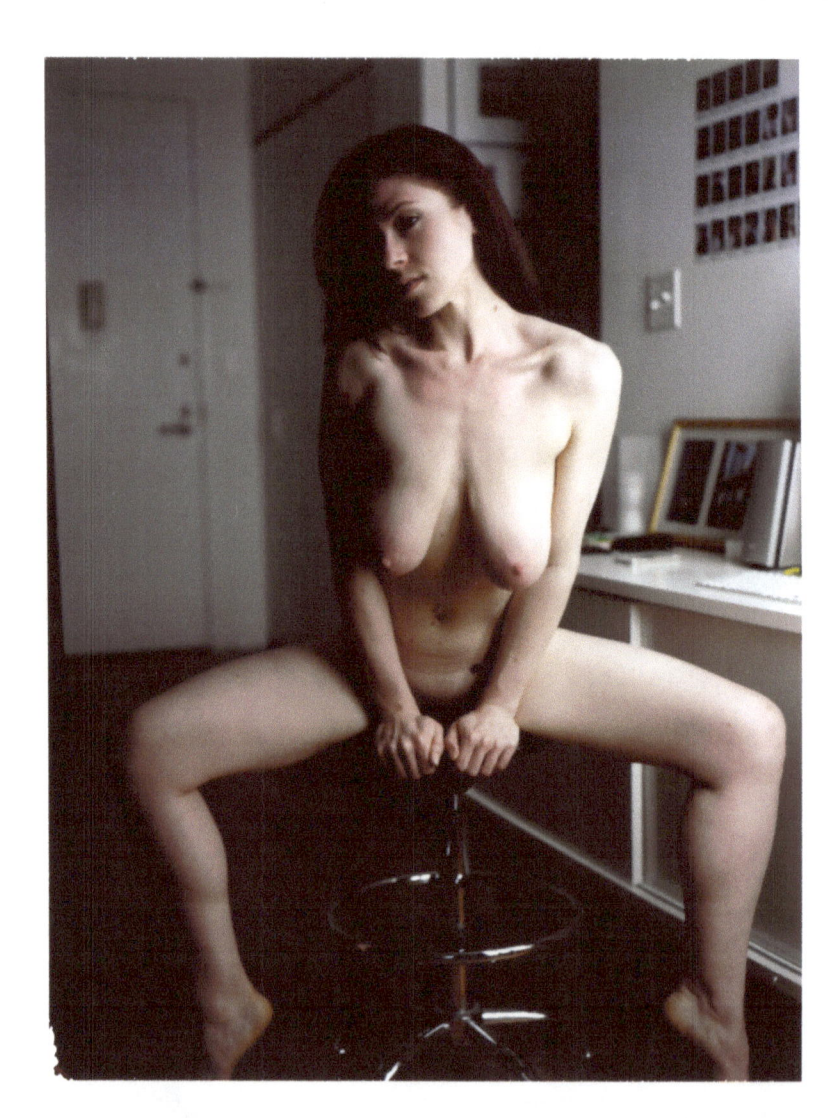

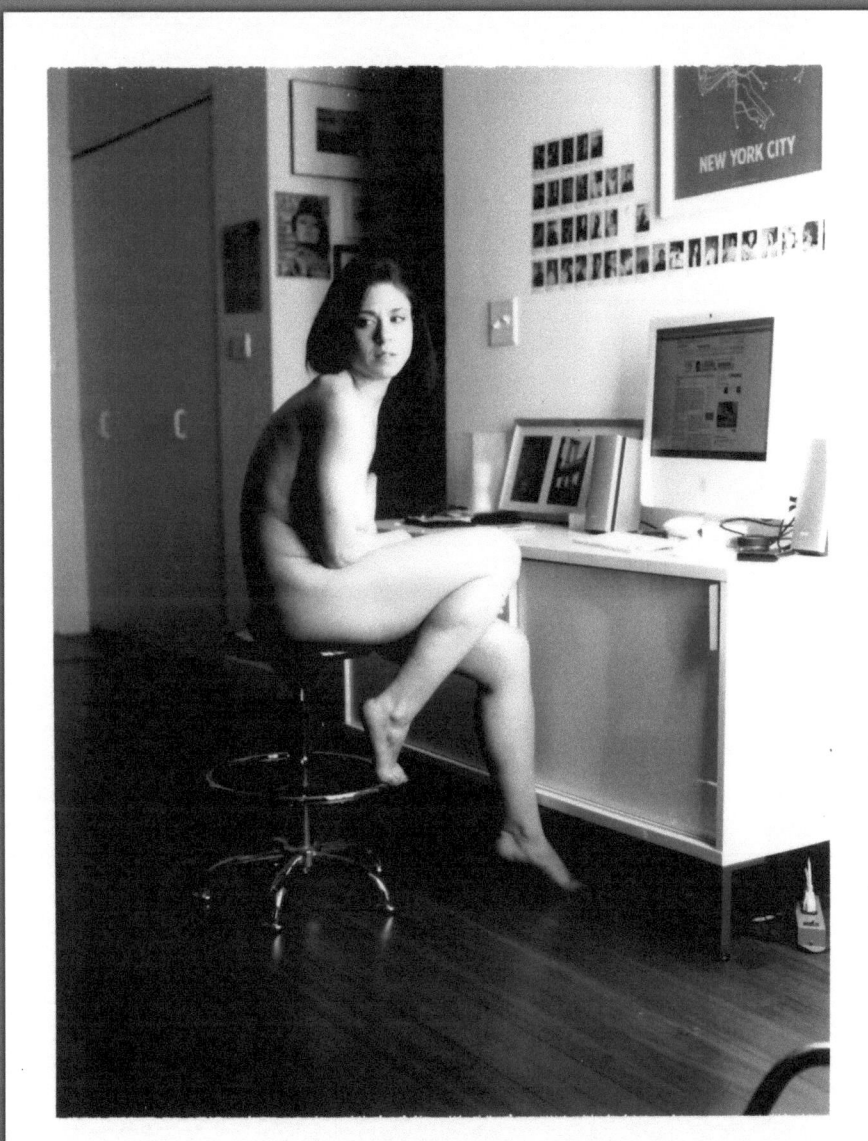

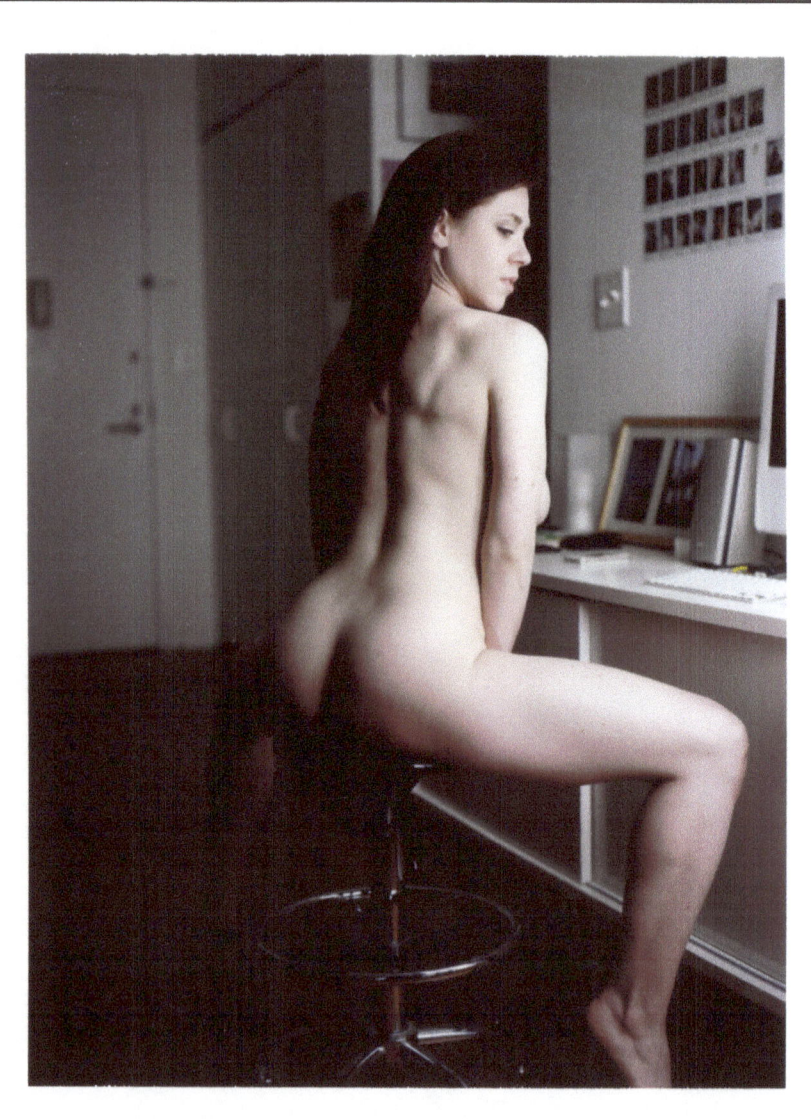

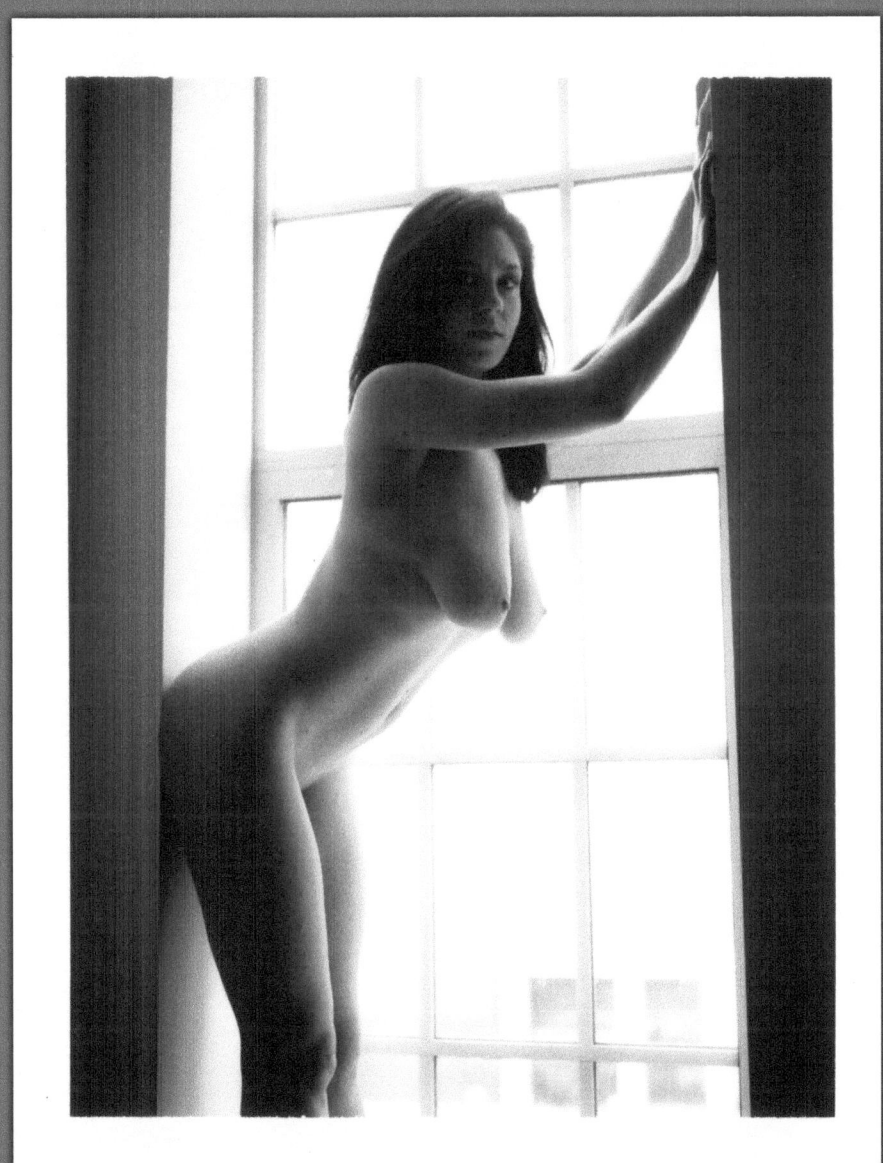

Elena

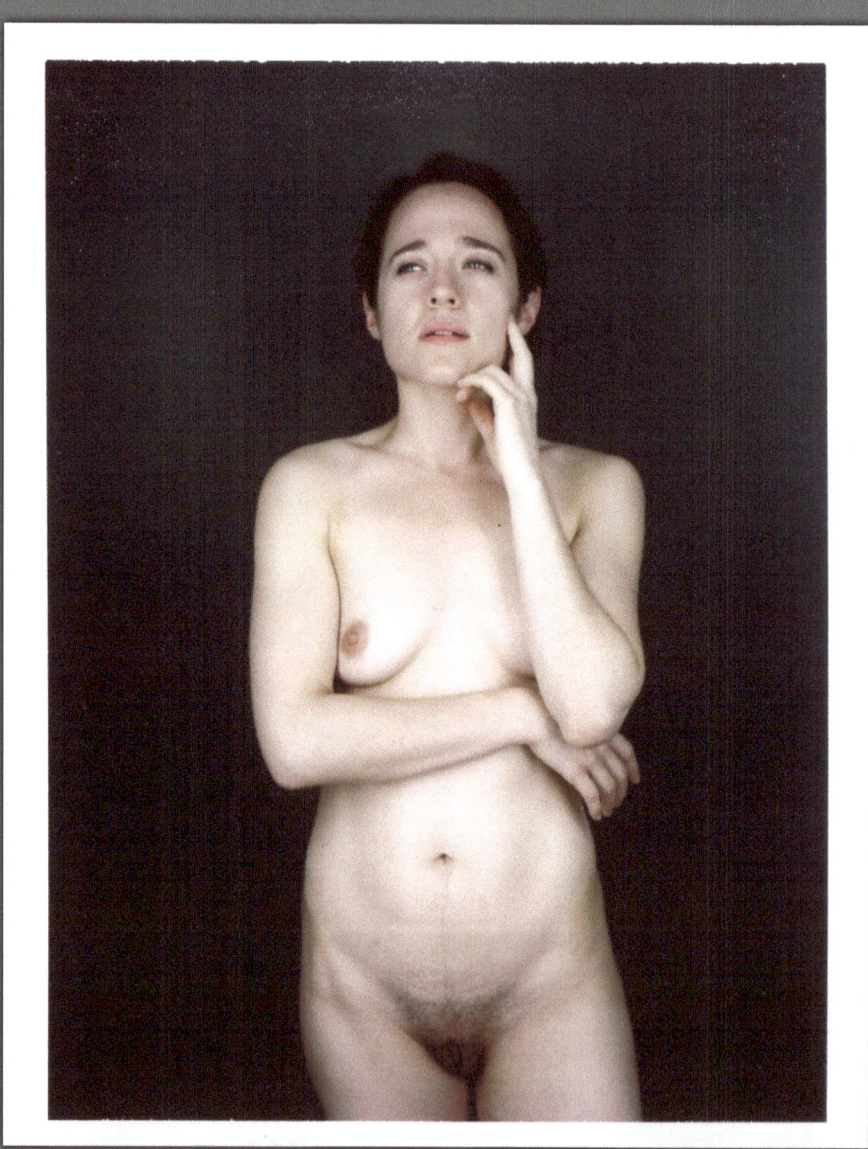

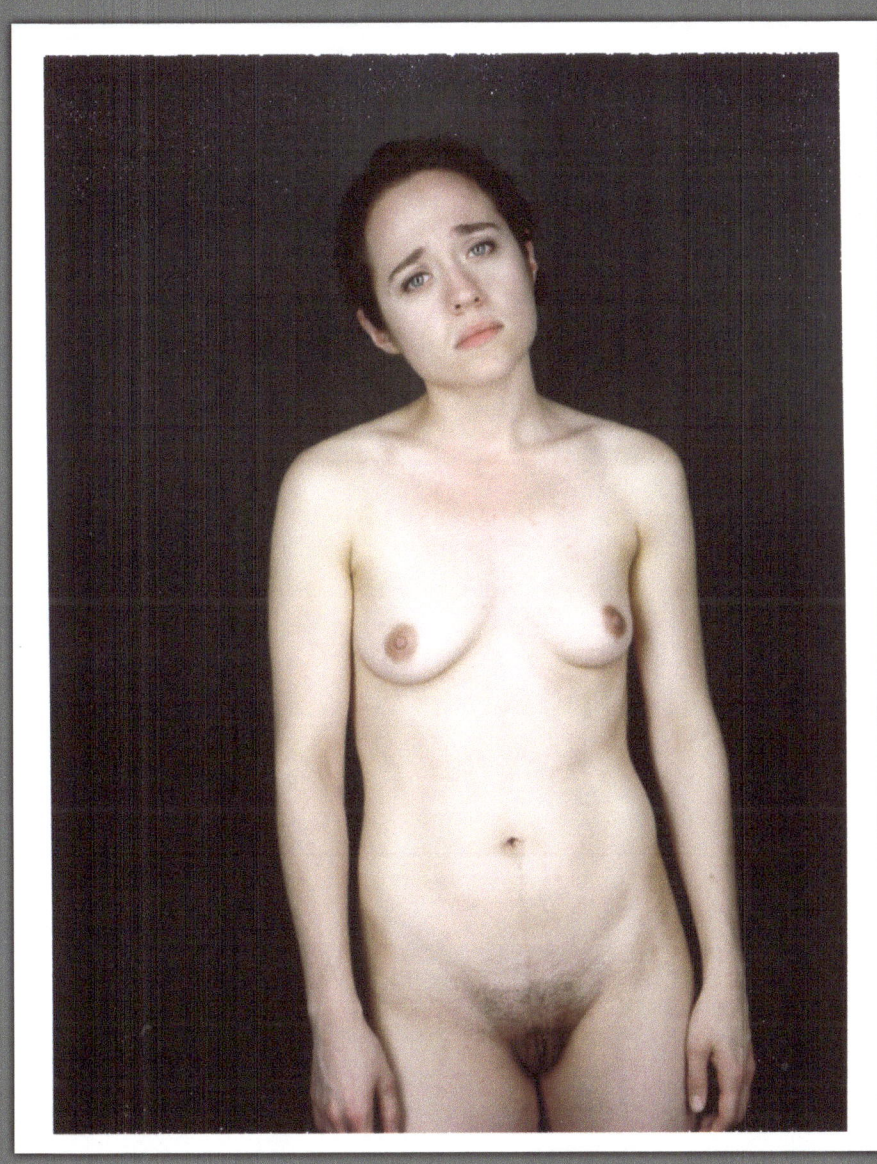

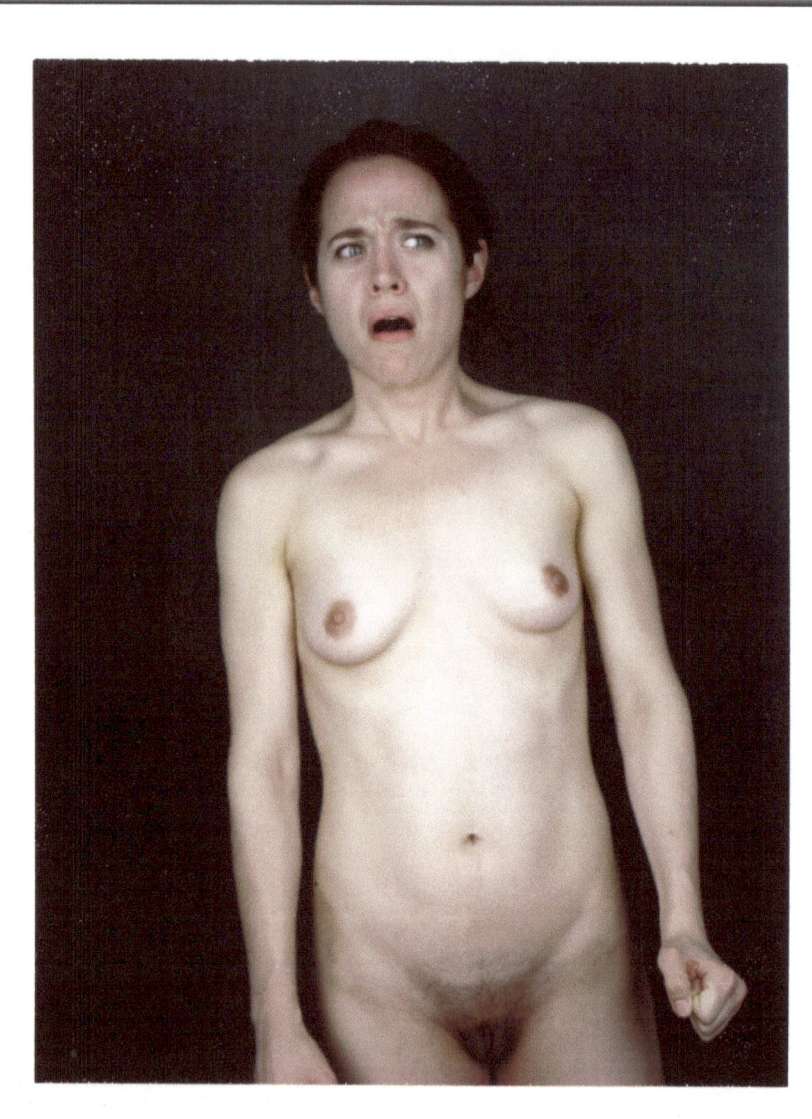

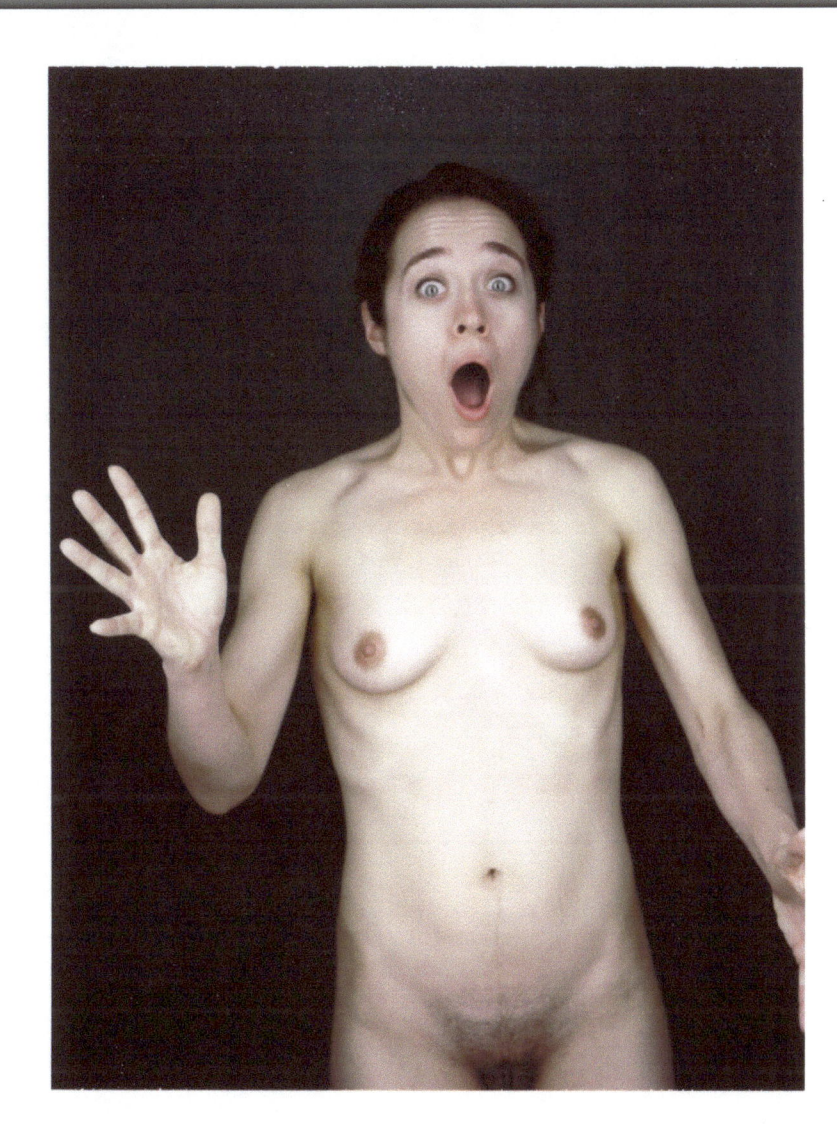

Erica Jay

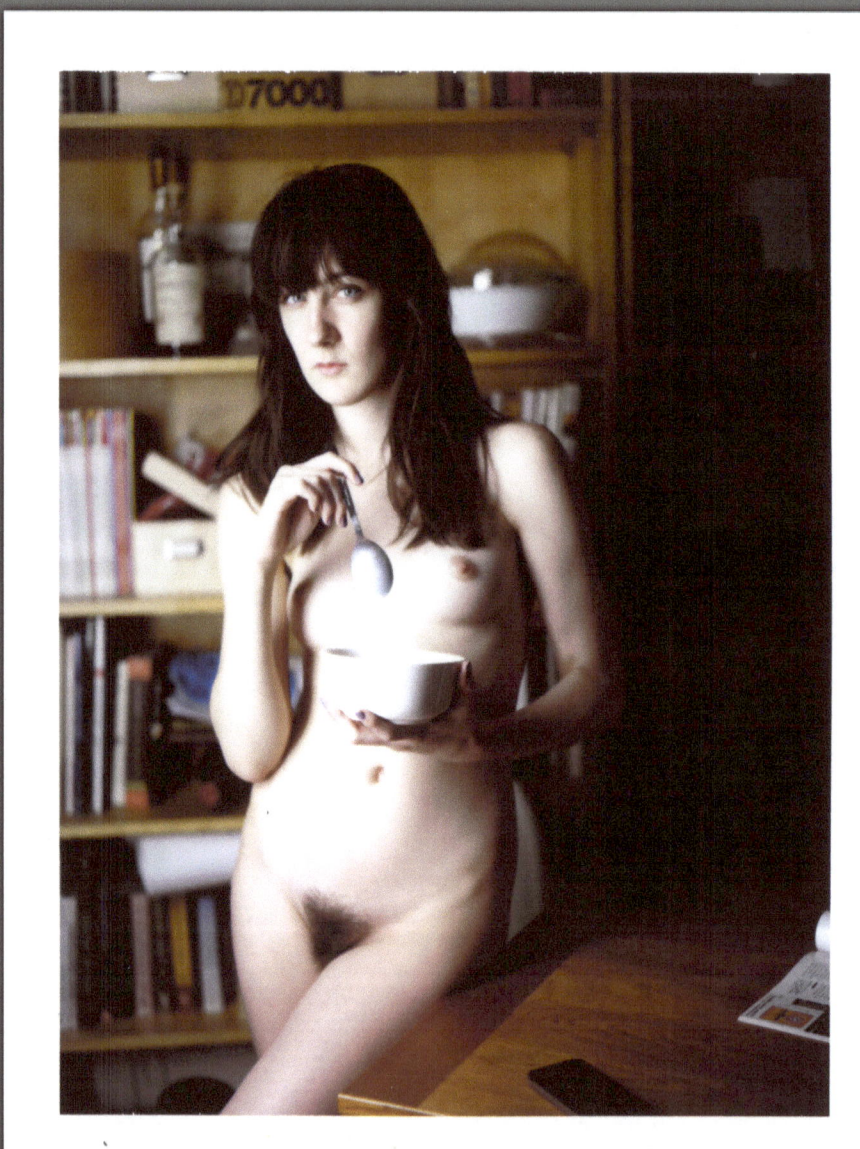

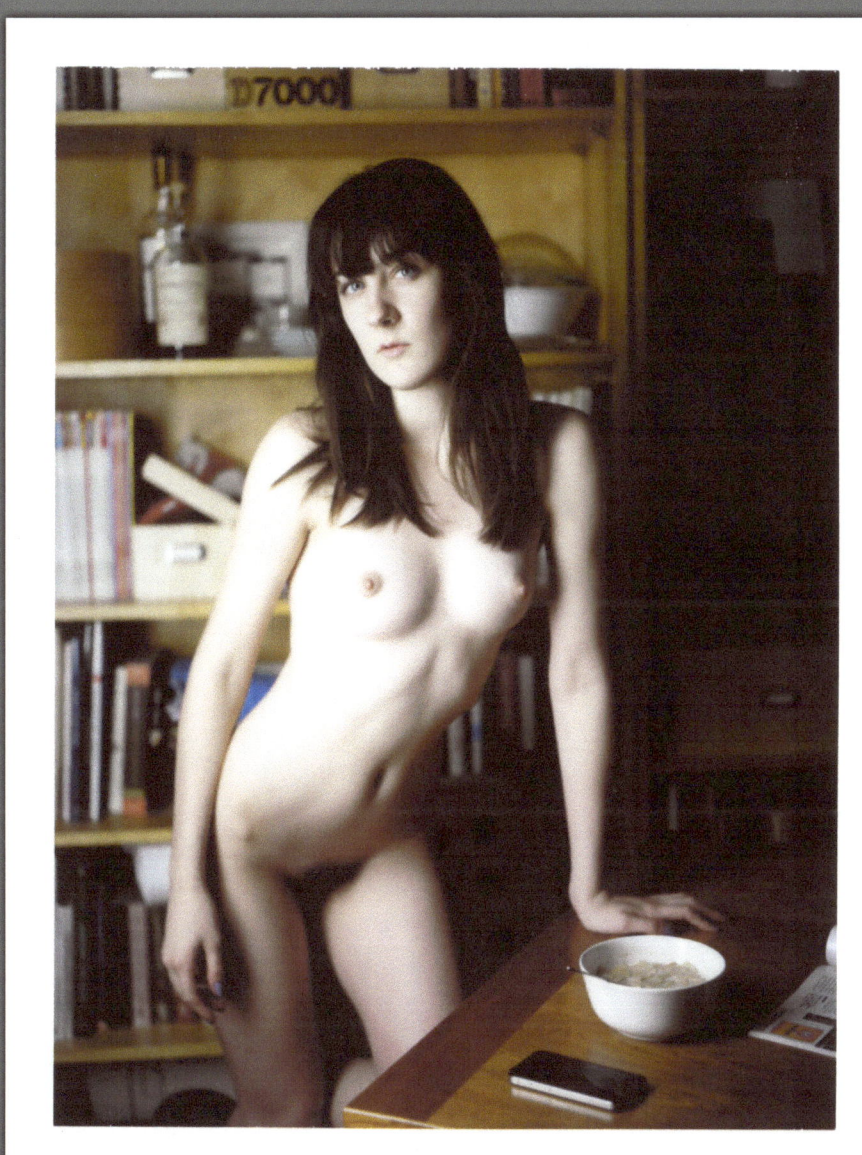

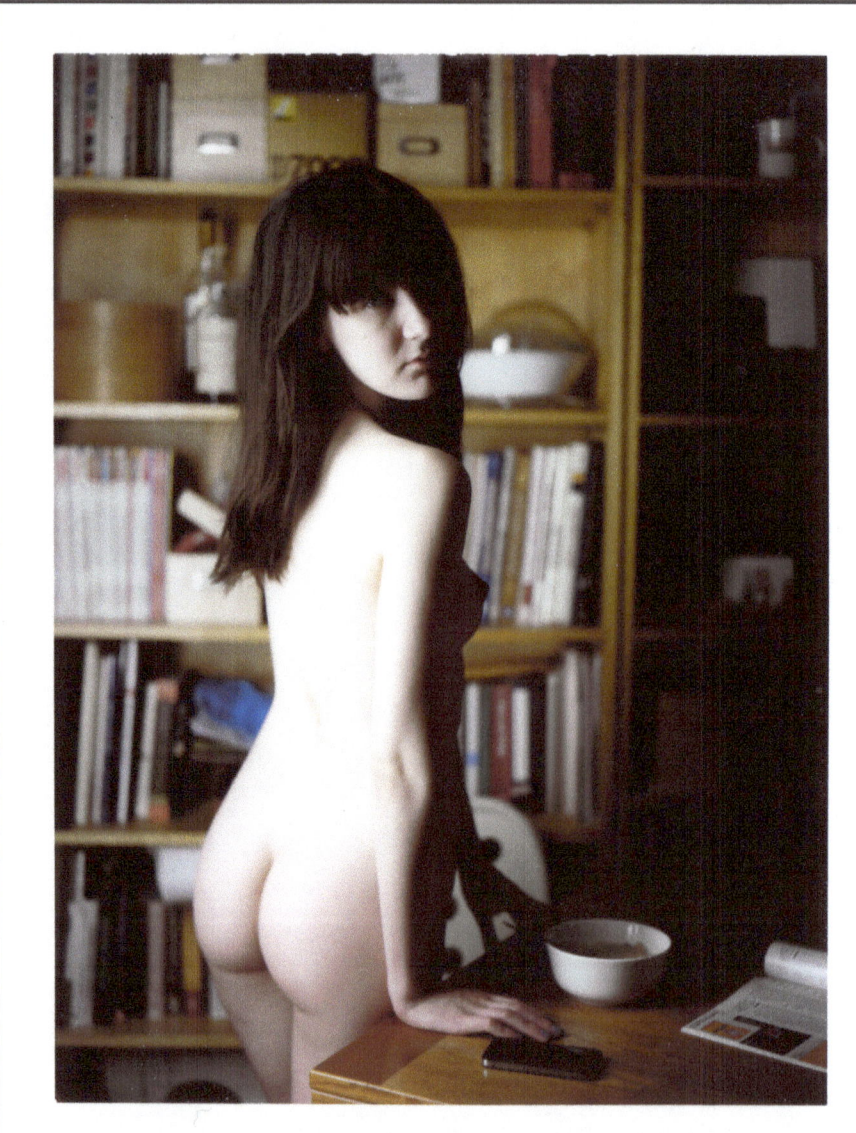

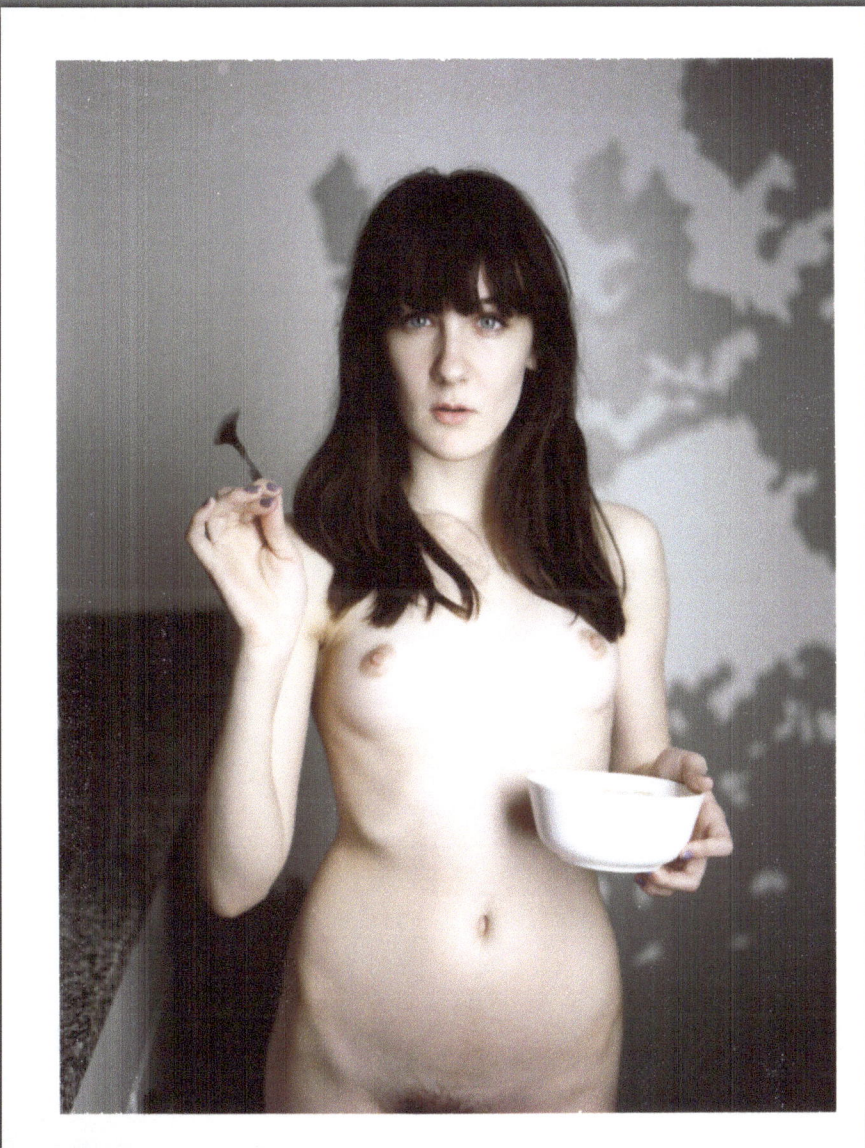

Alexis

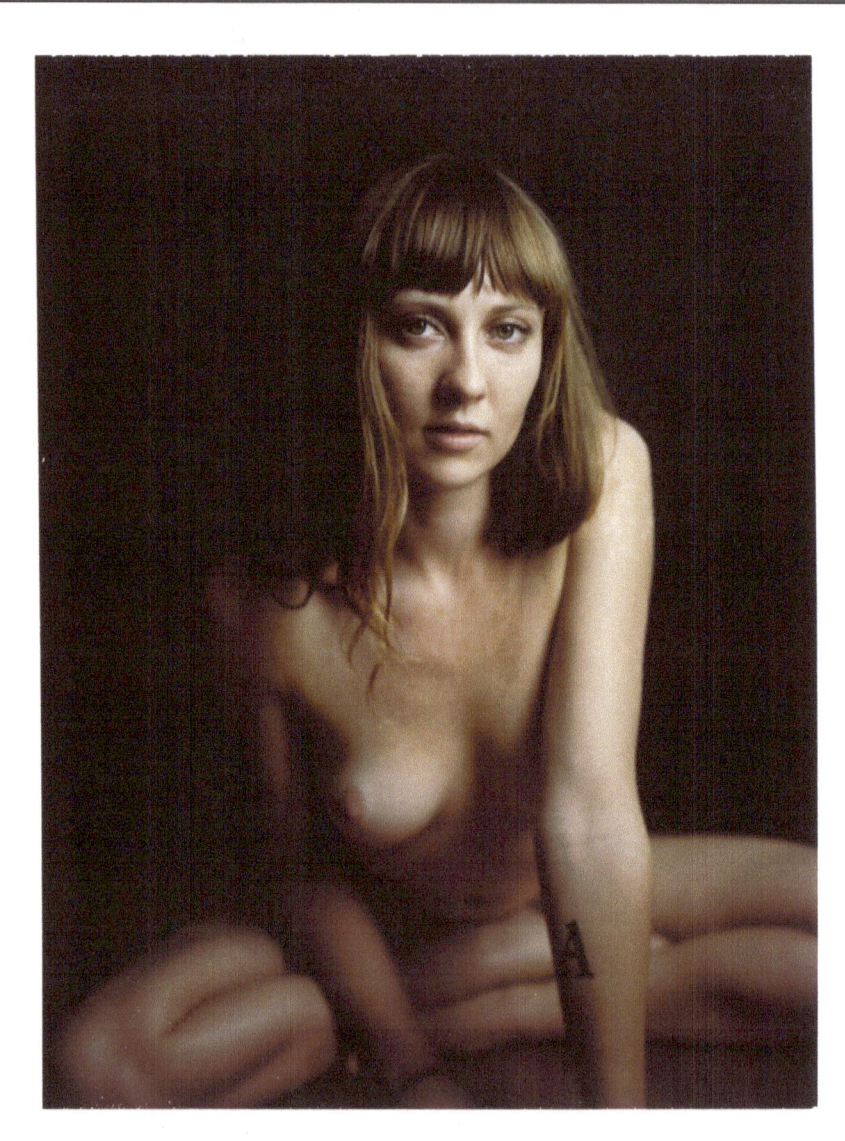

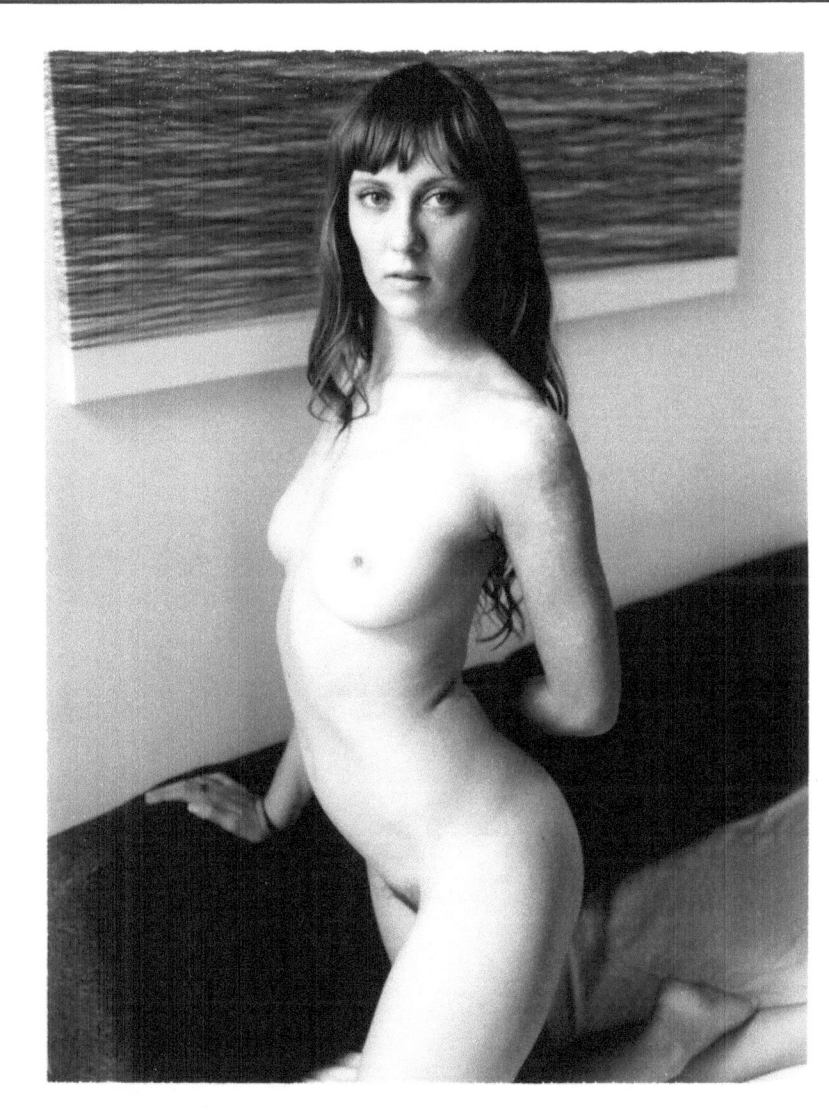

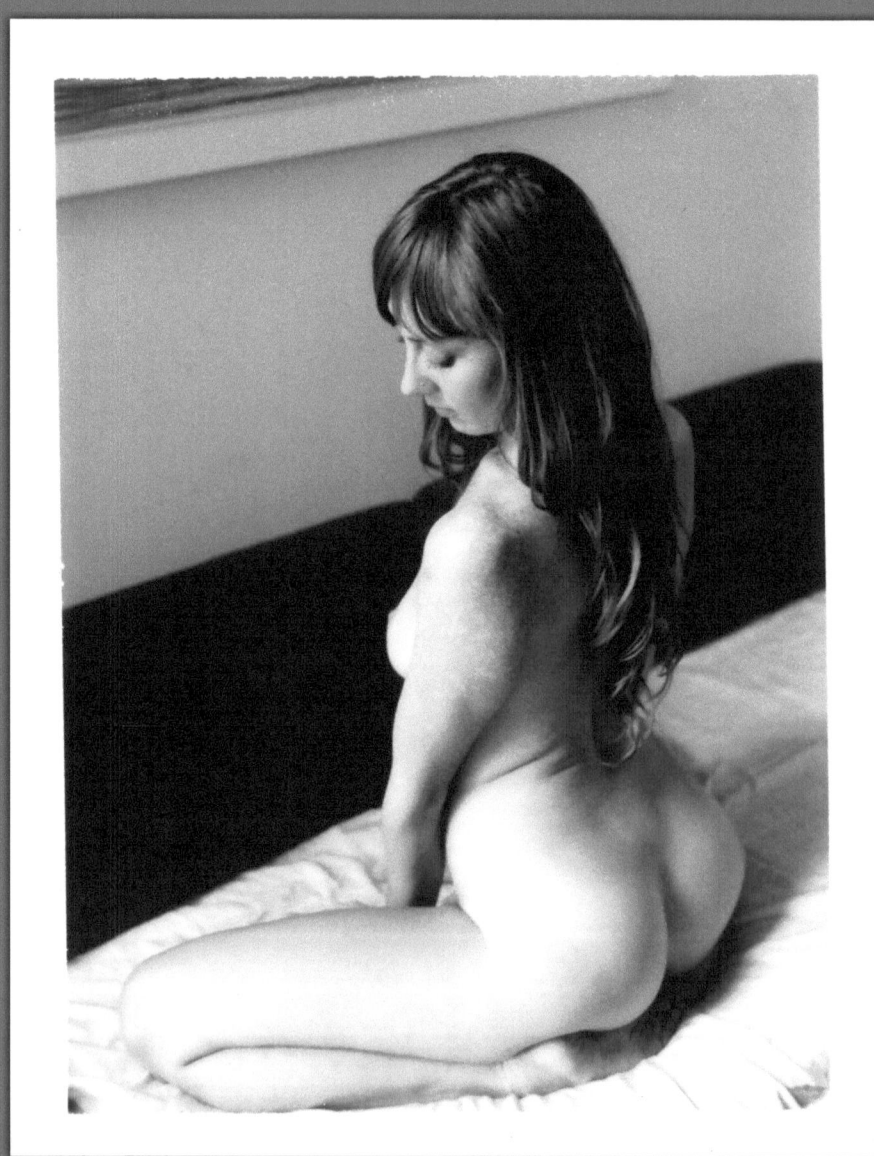

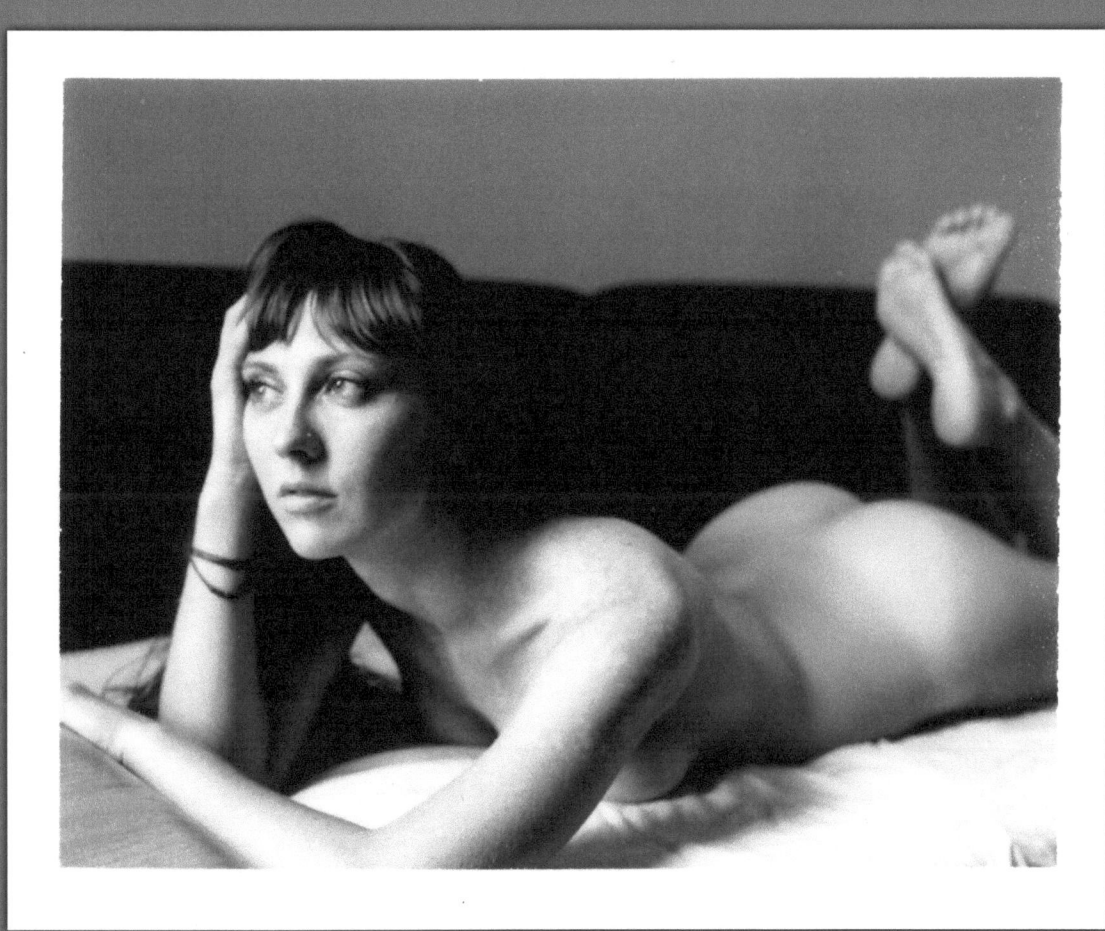

Lindsay

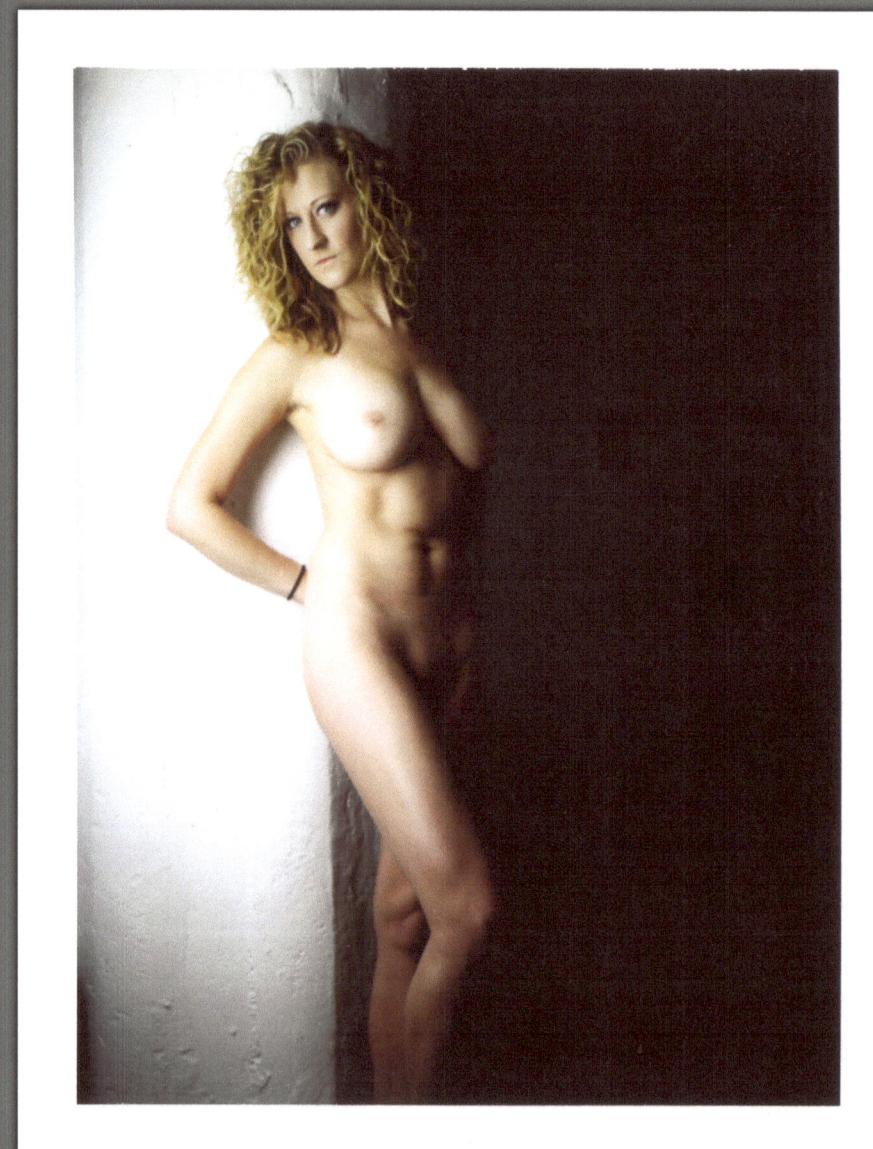

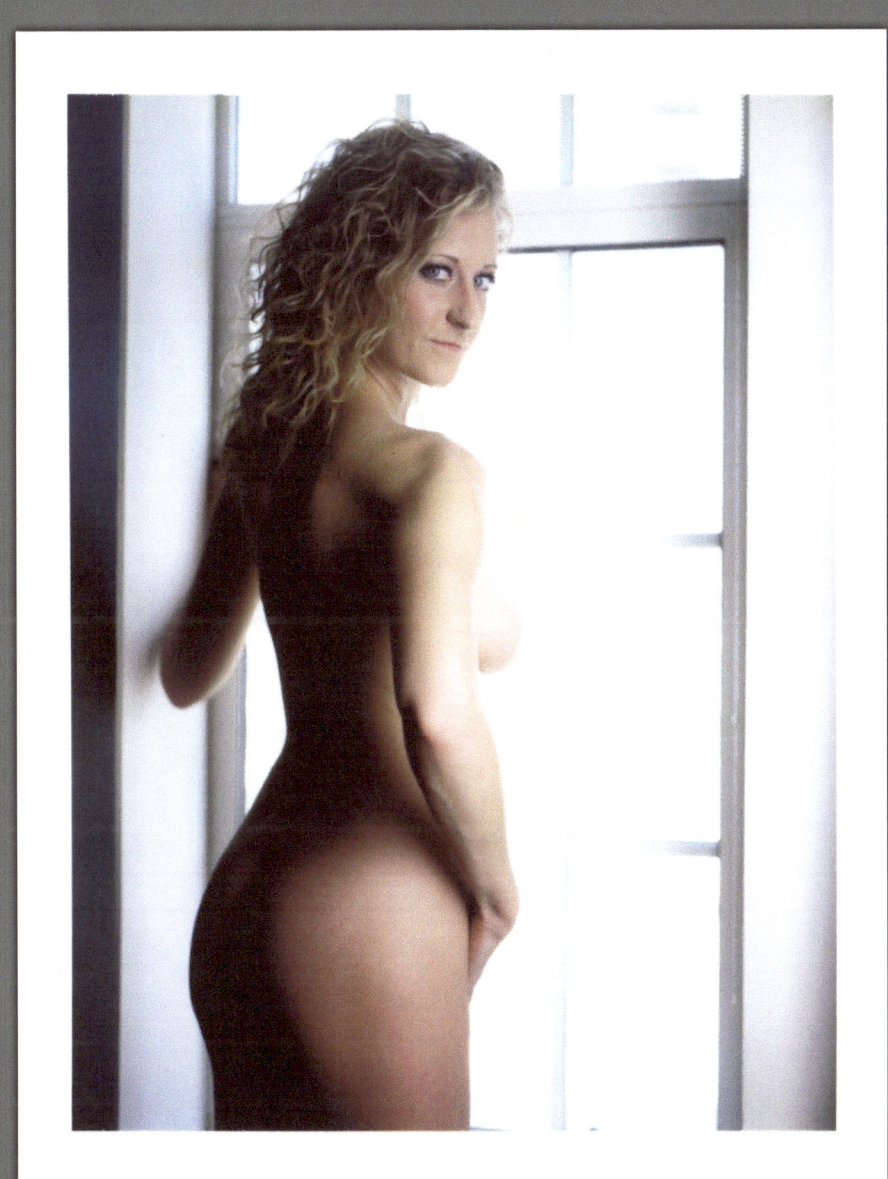

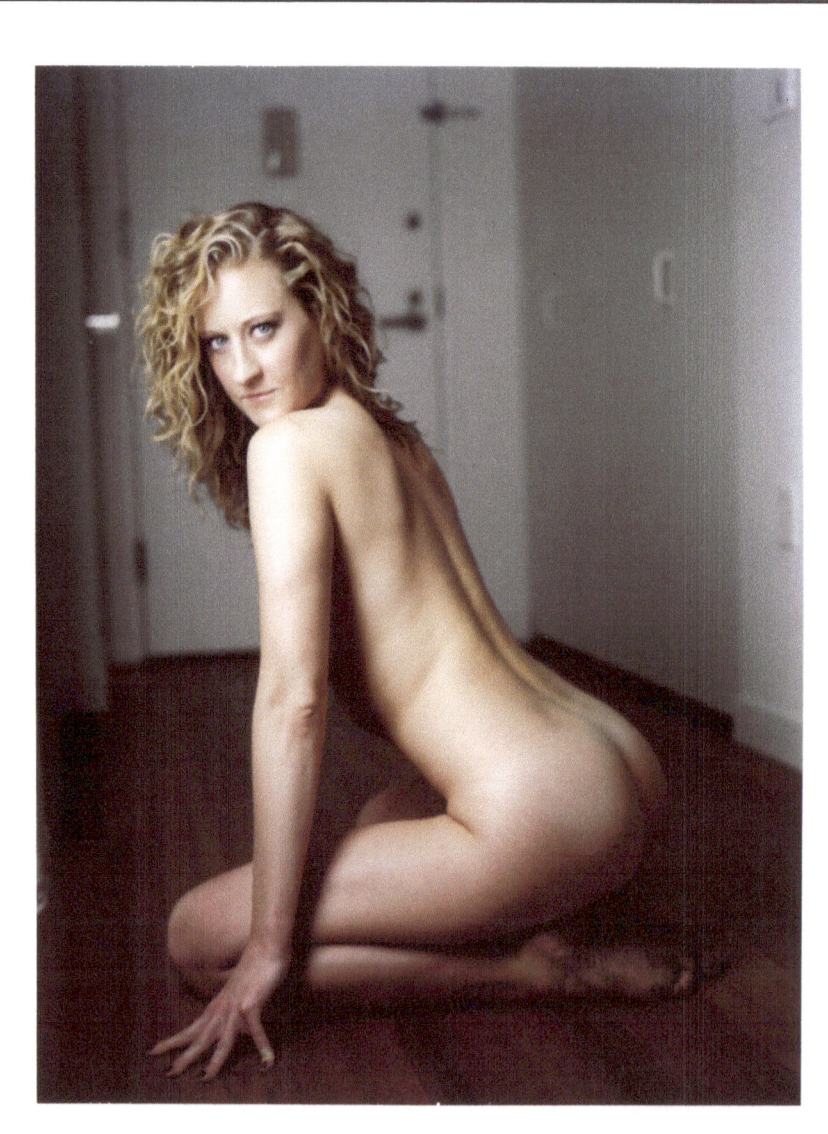

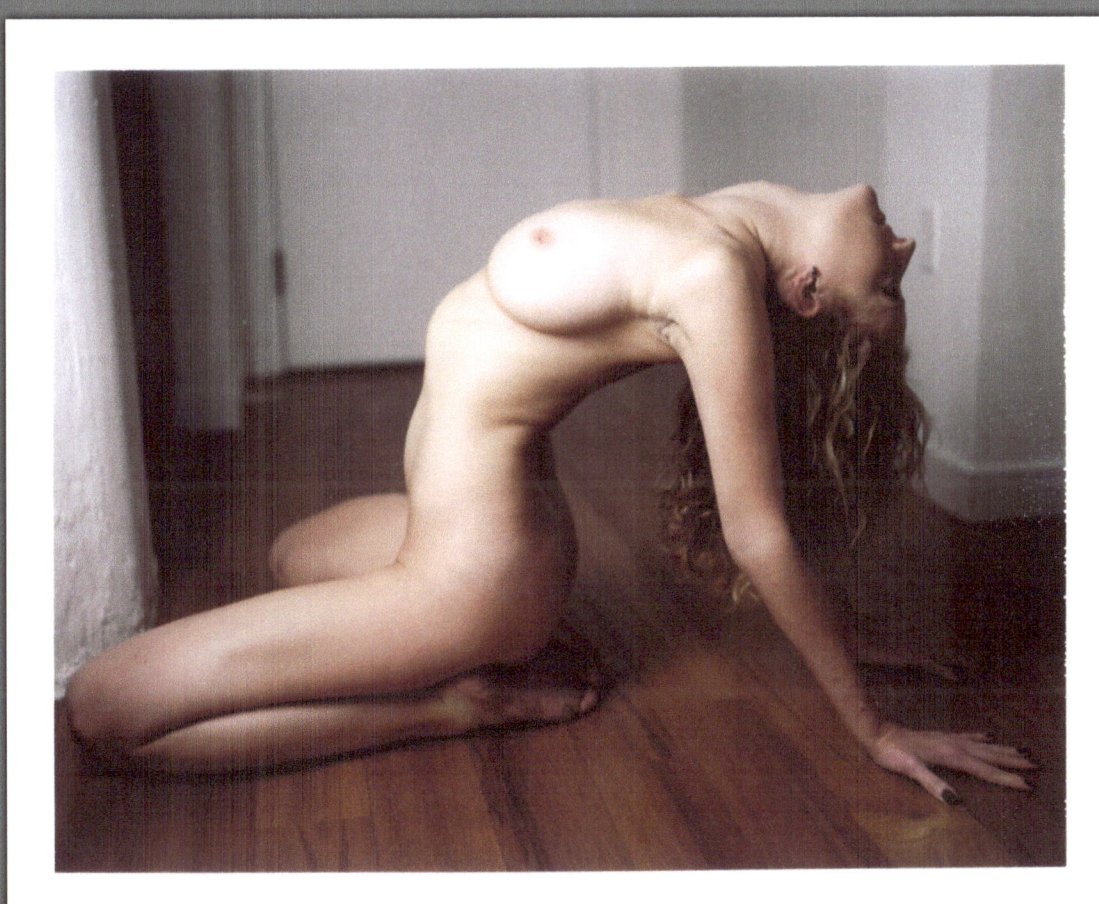

Anna

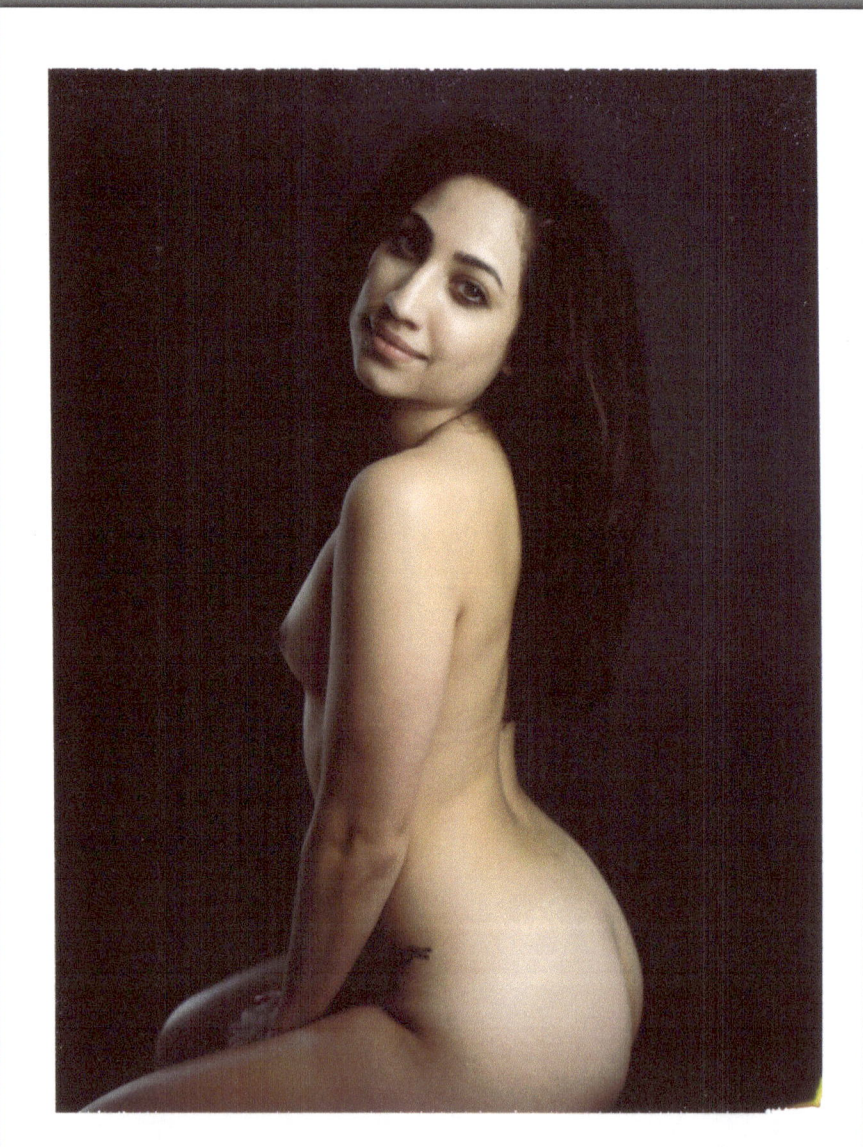

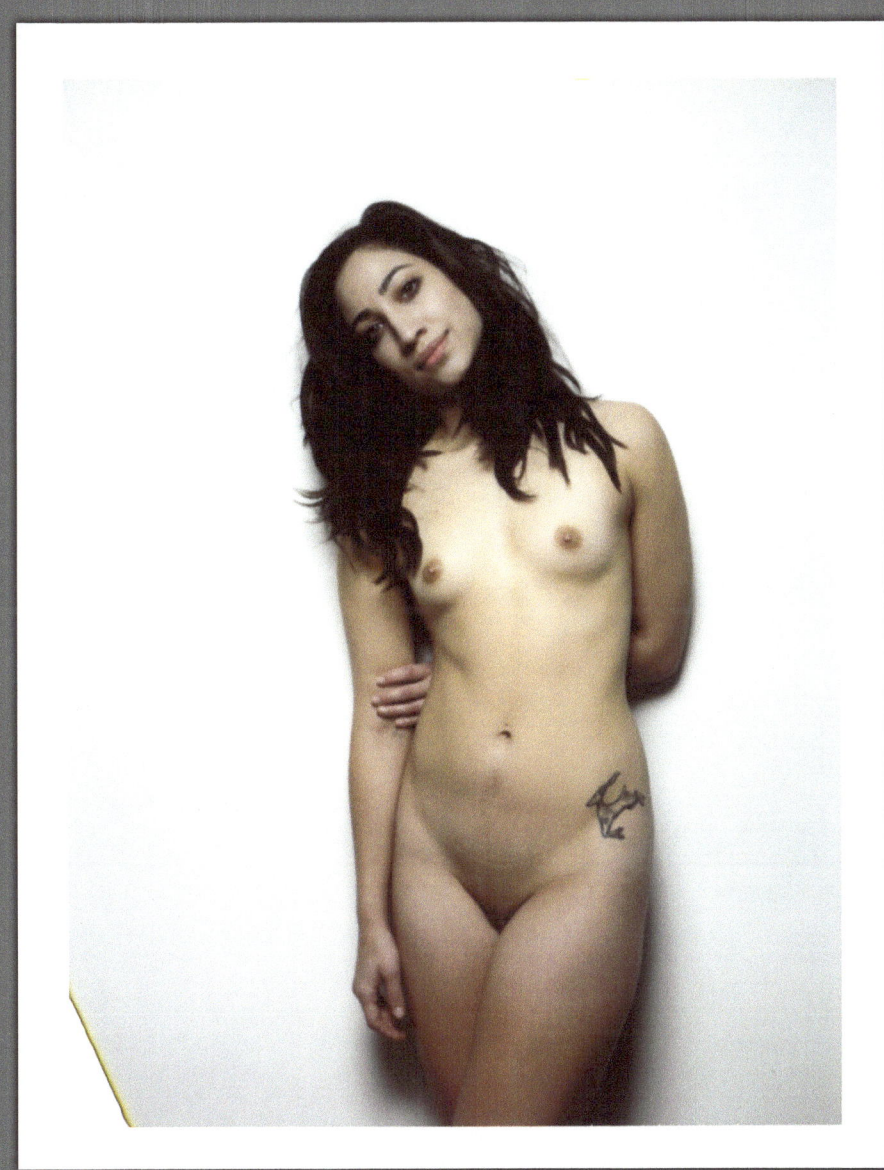

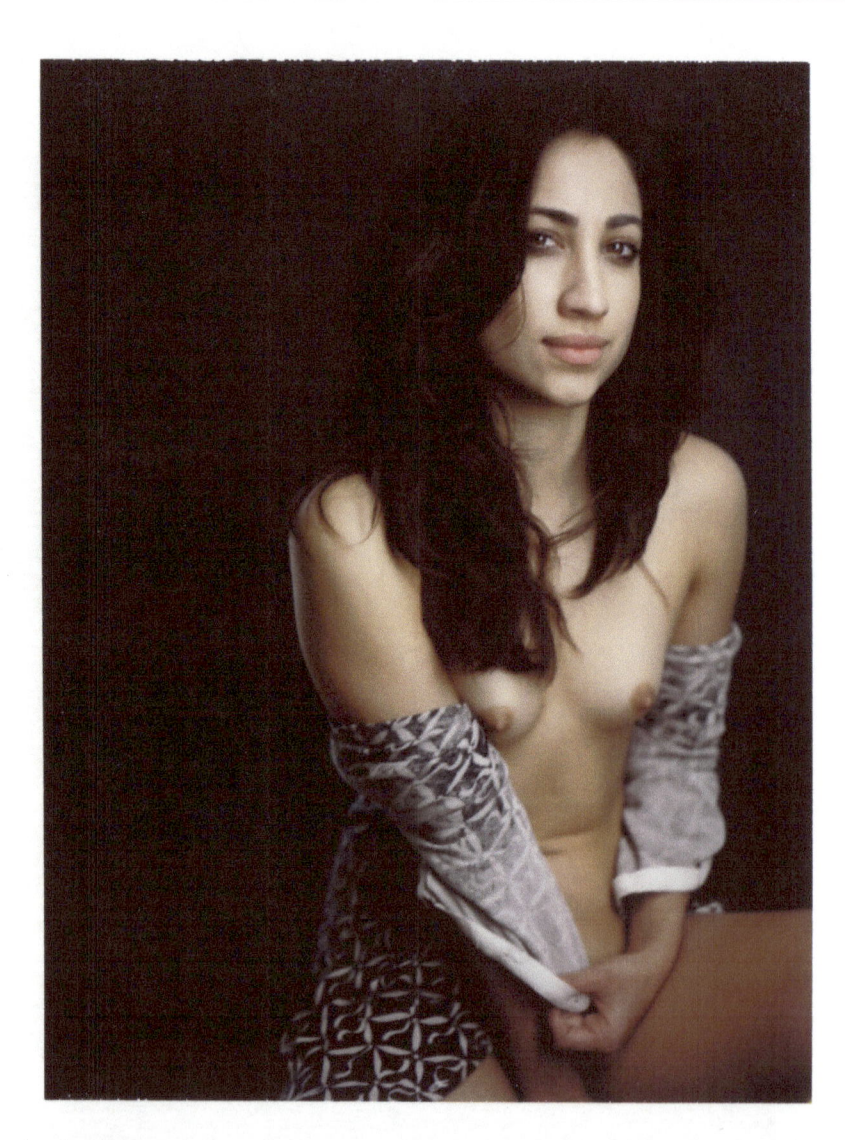

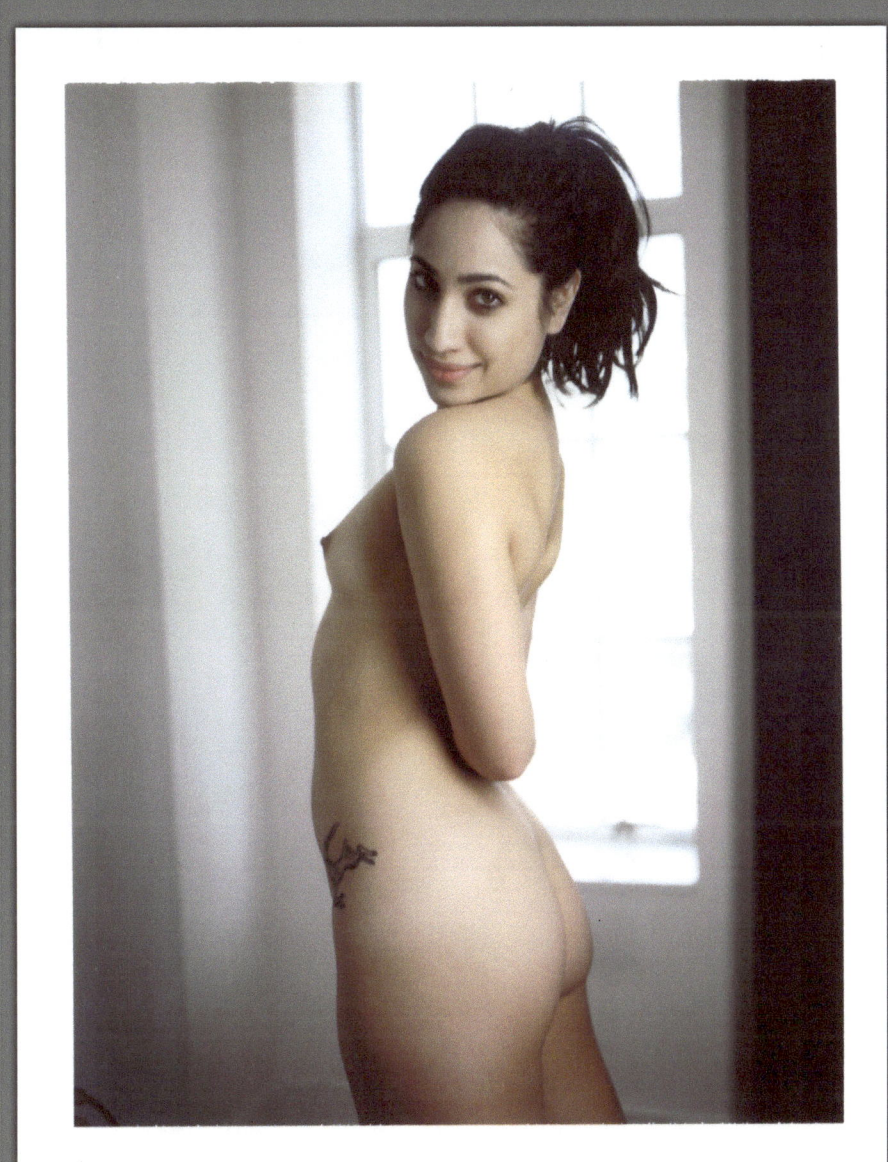

Maggie

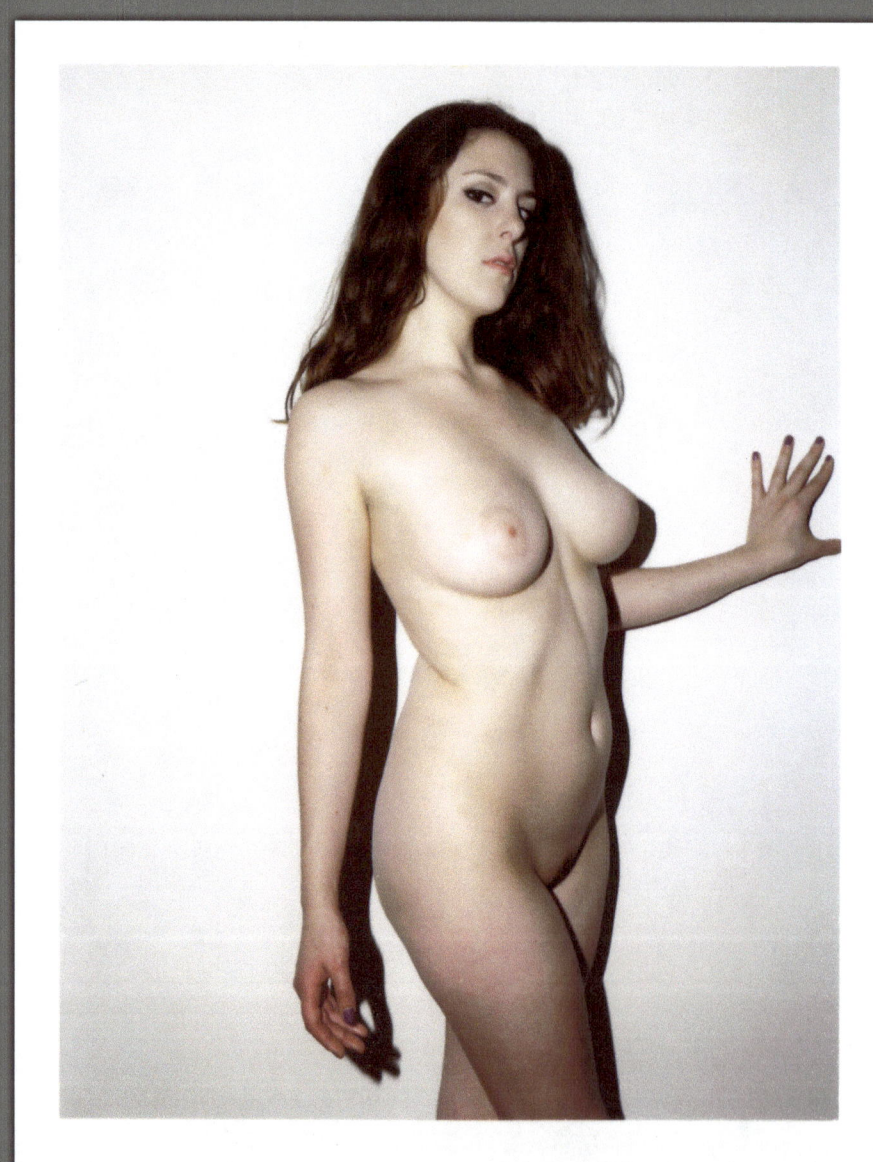

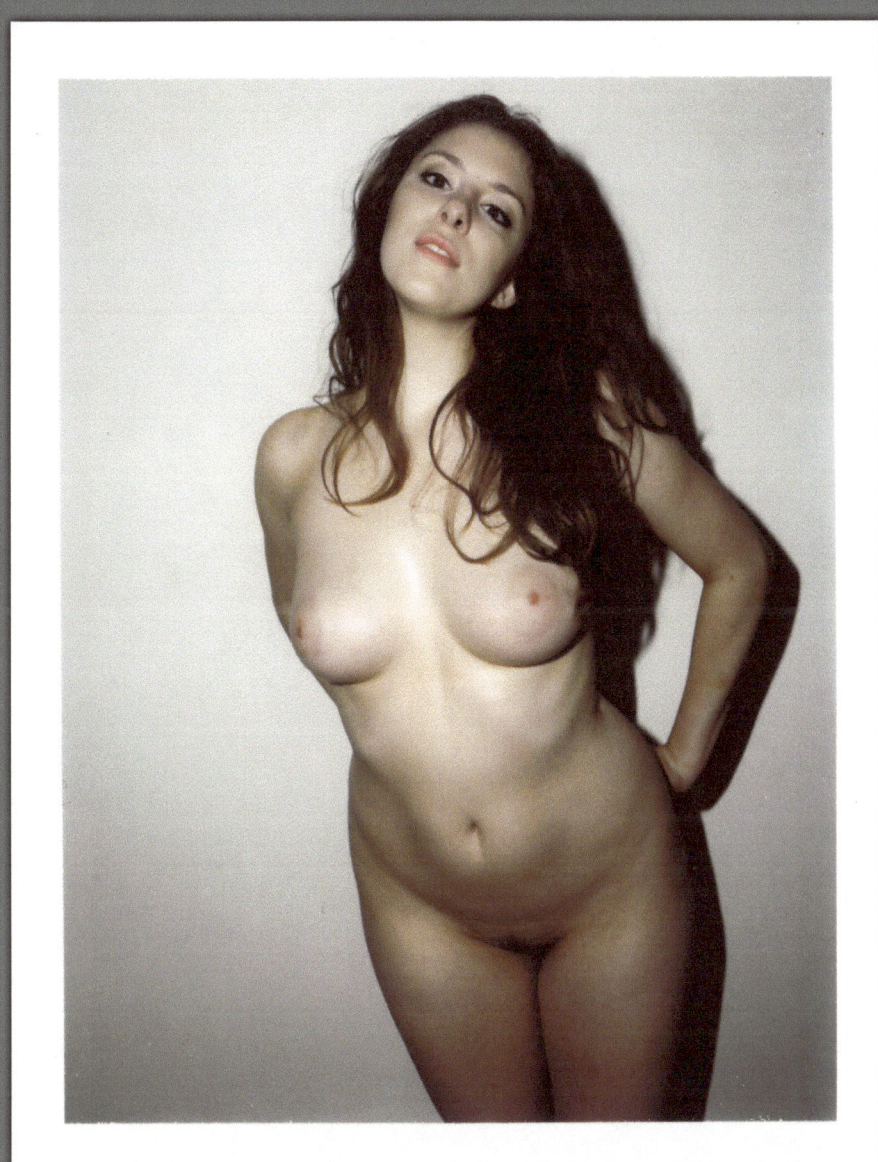

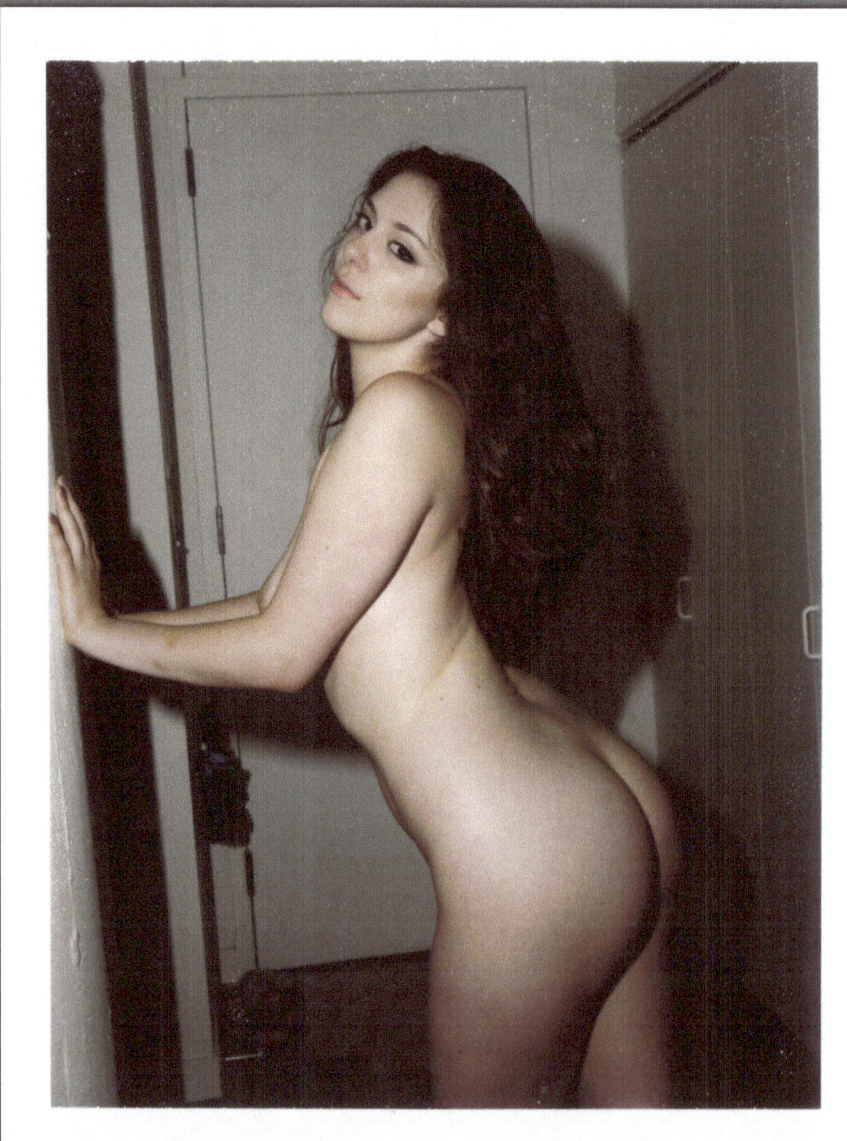

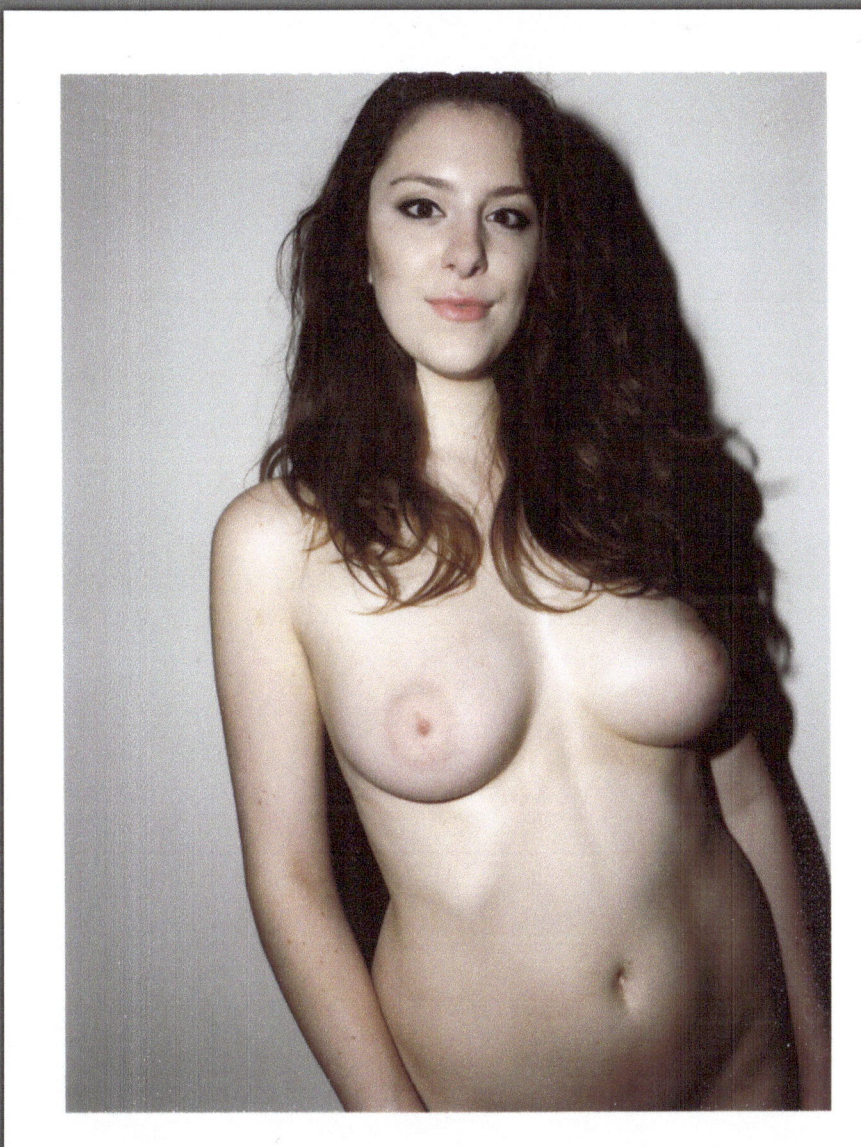

Wini

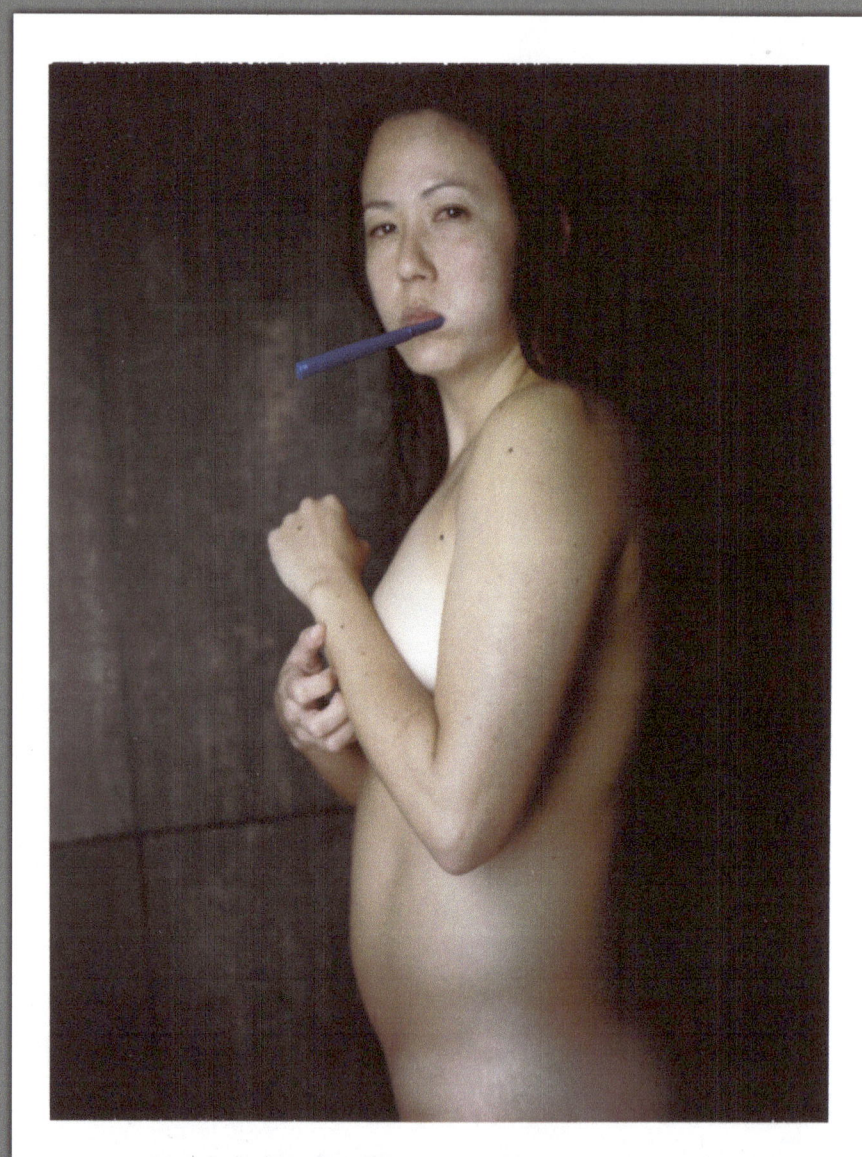

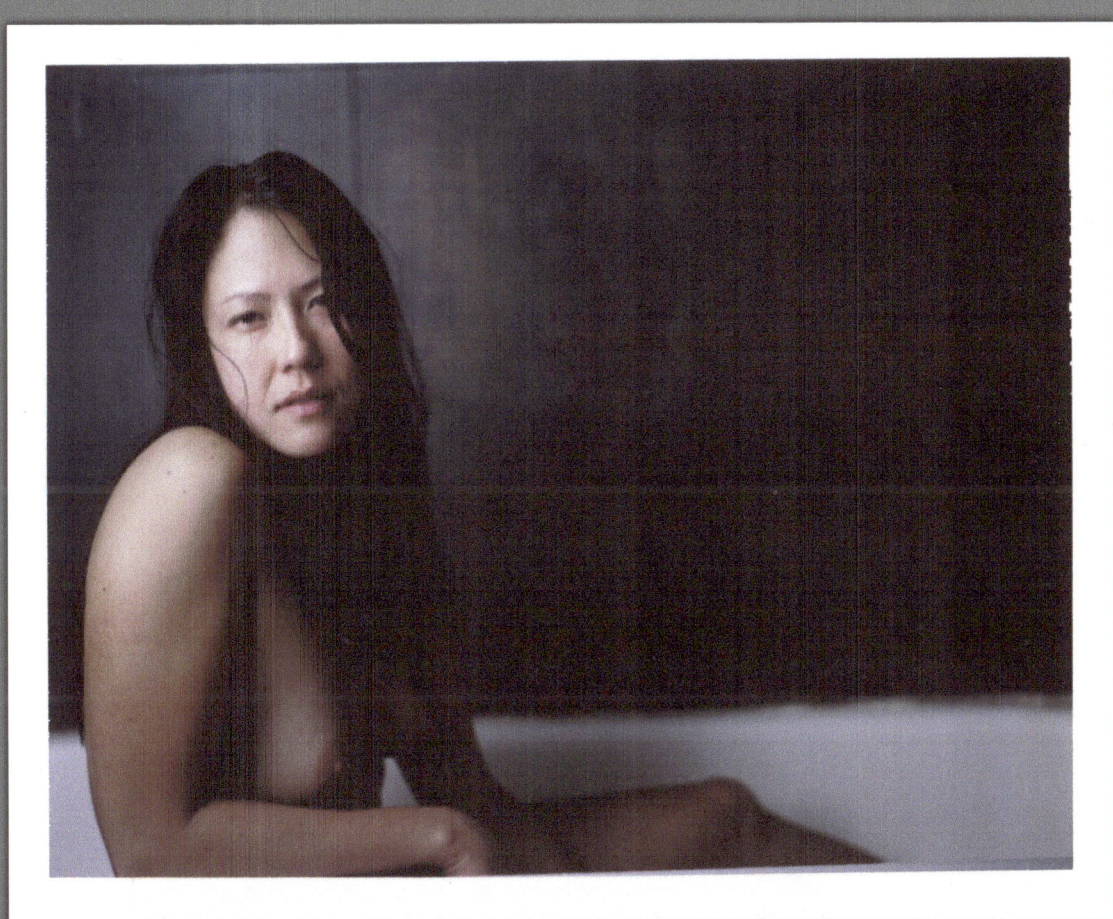

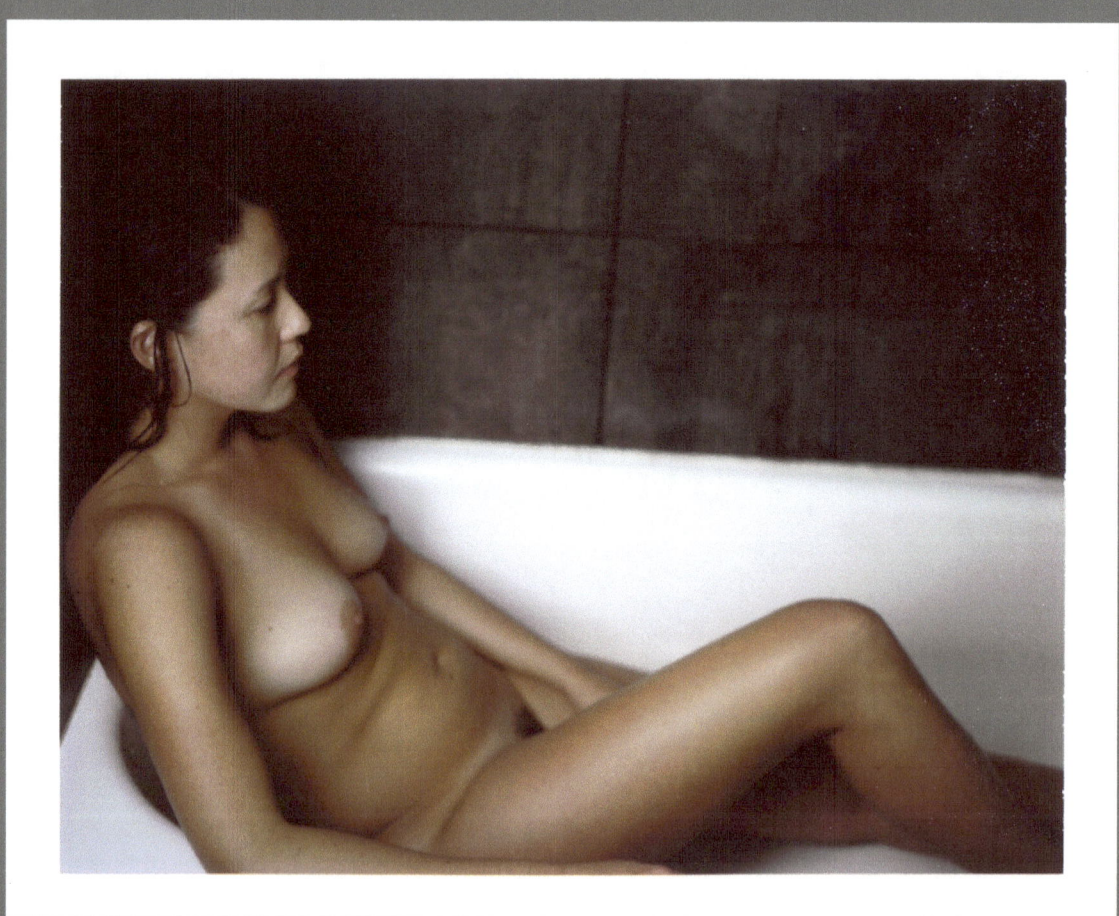

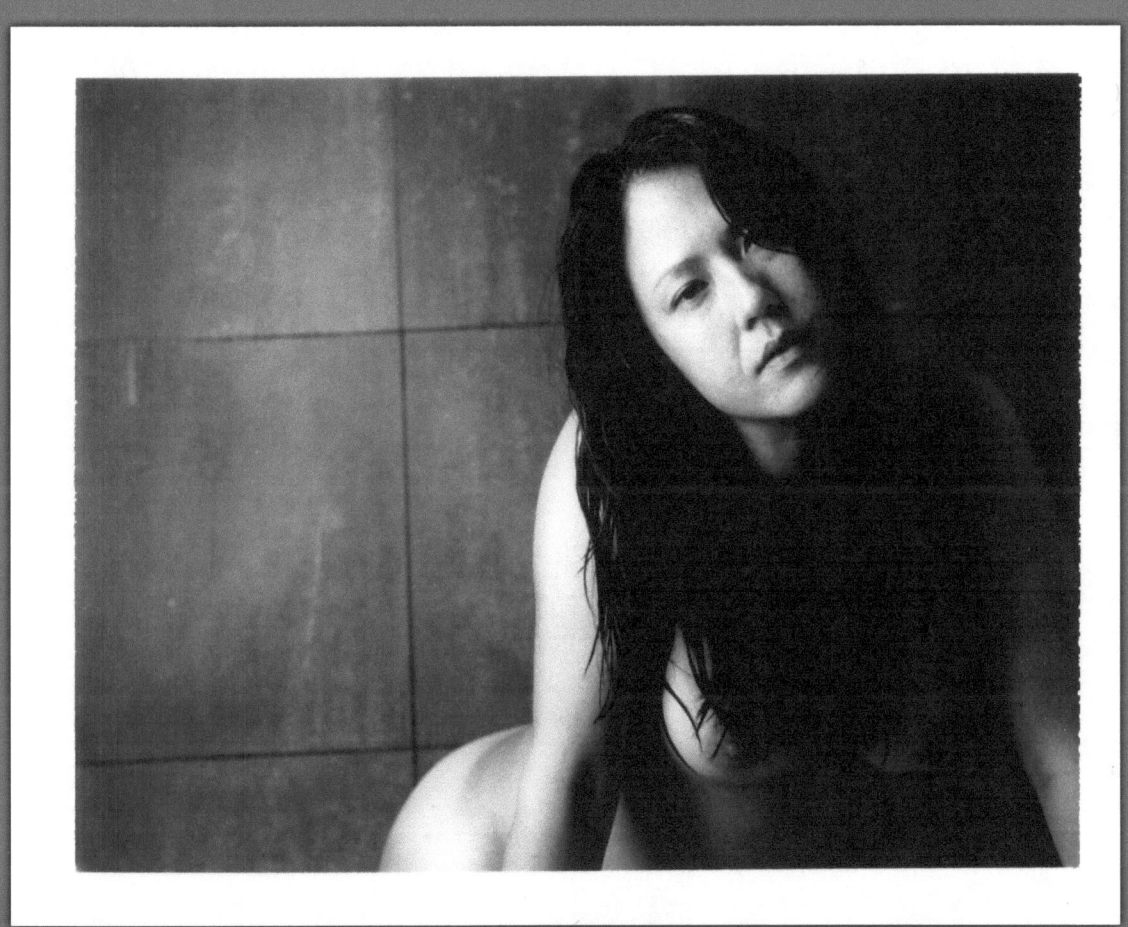

Eileen

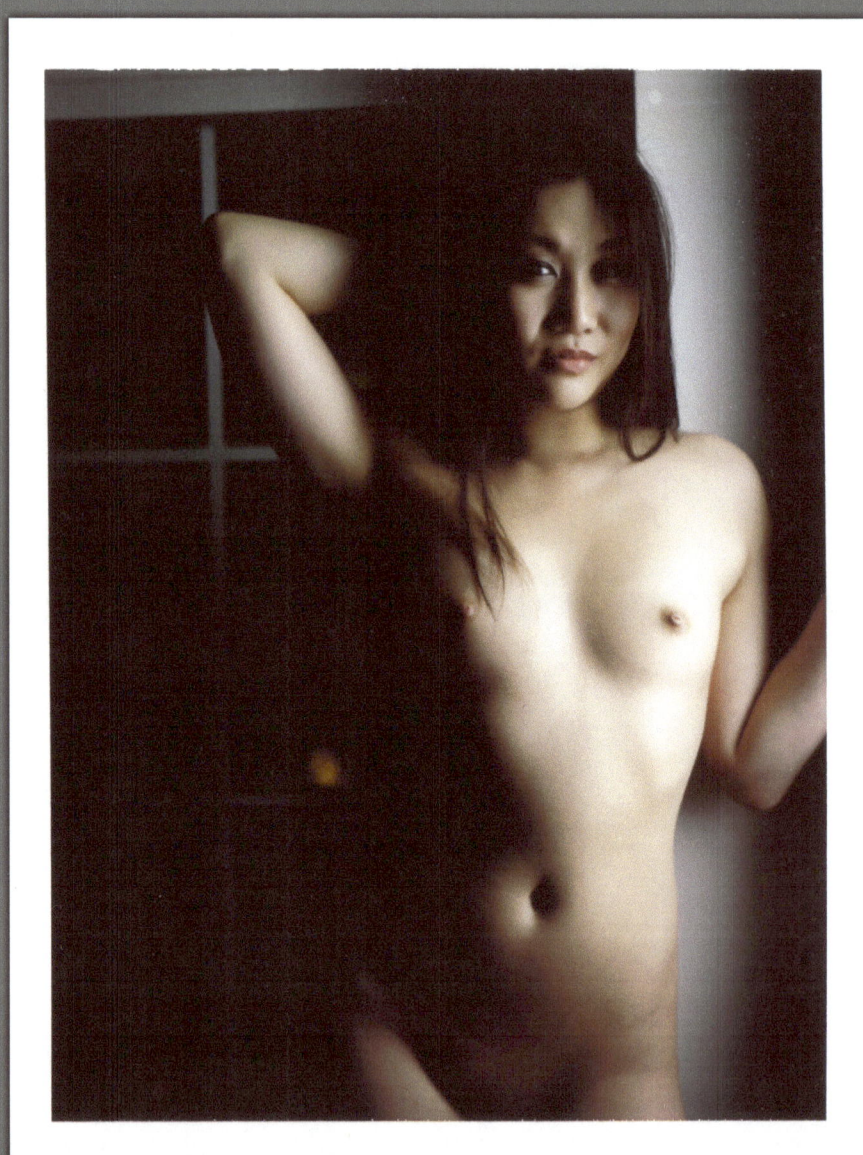

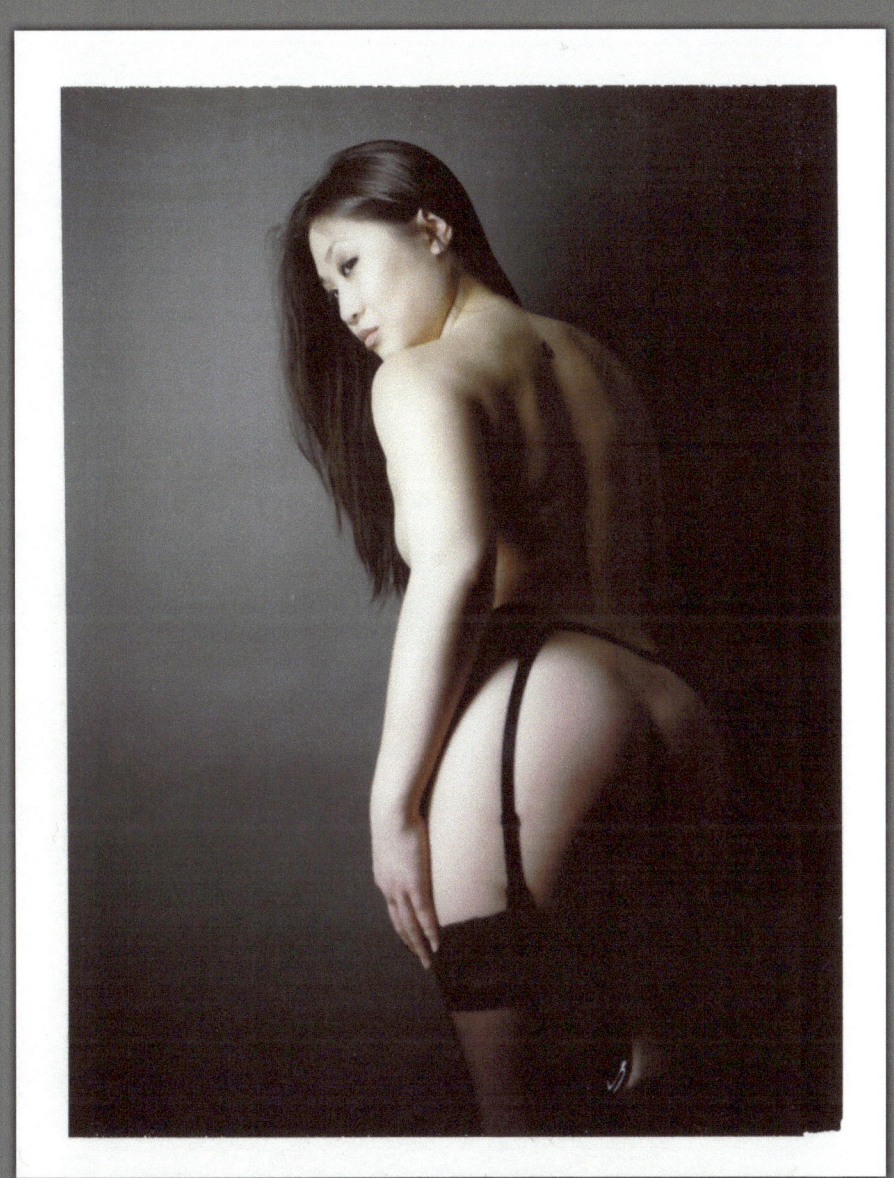

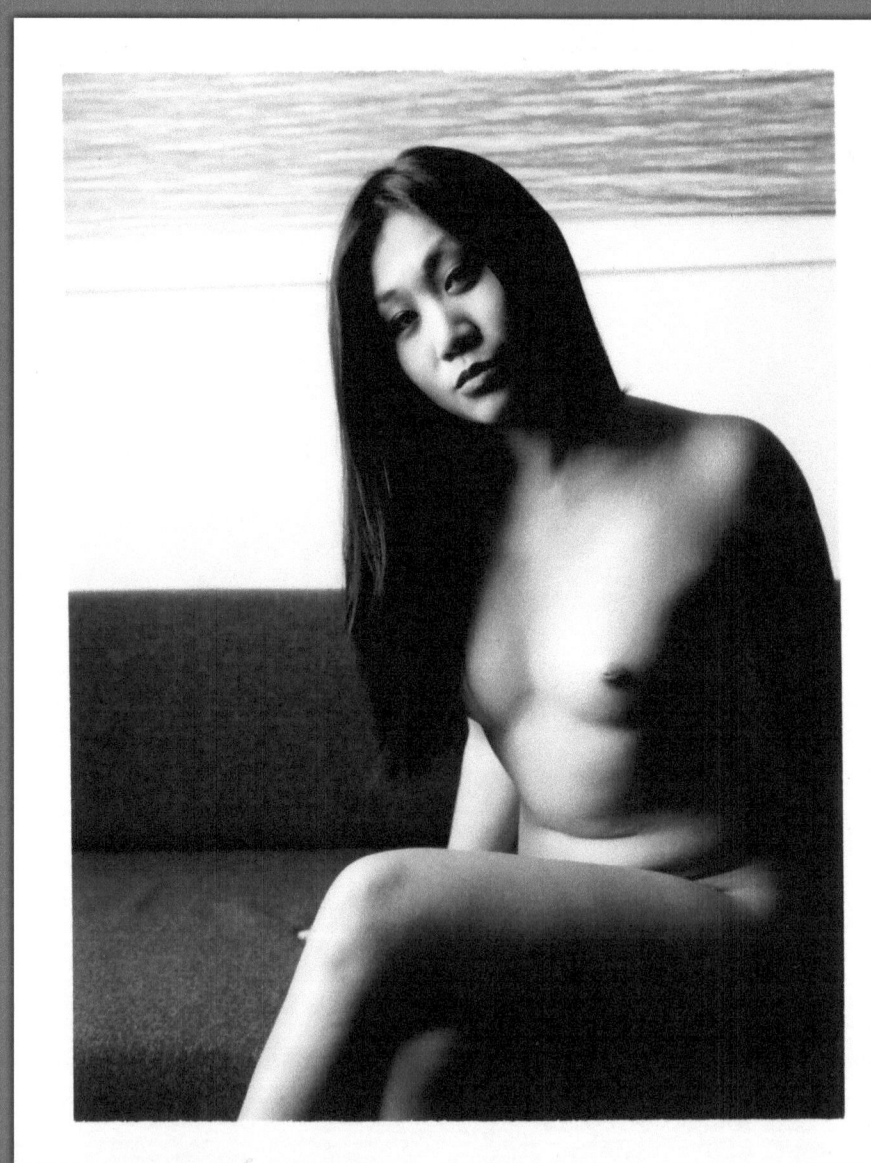

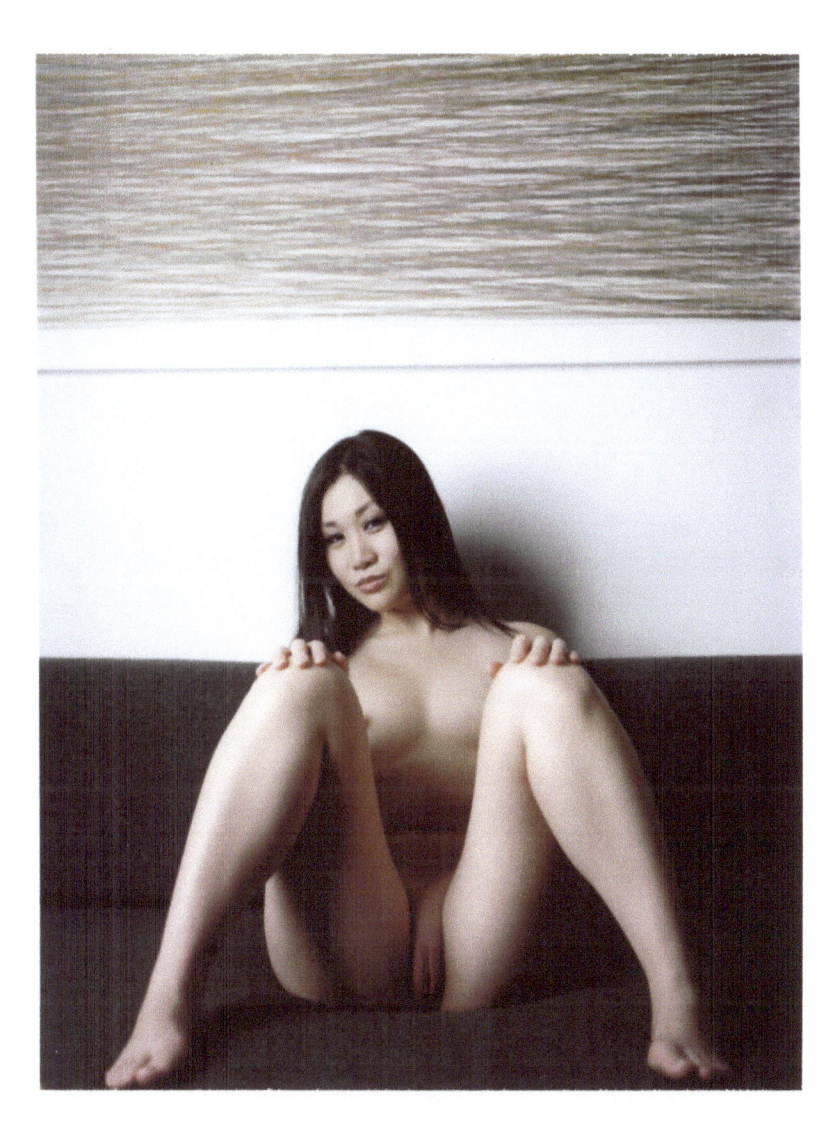

Michelle

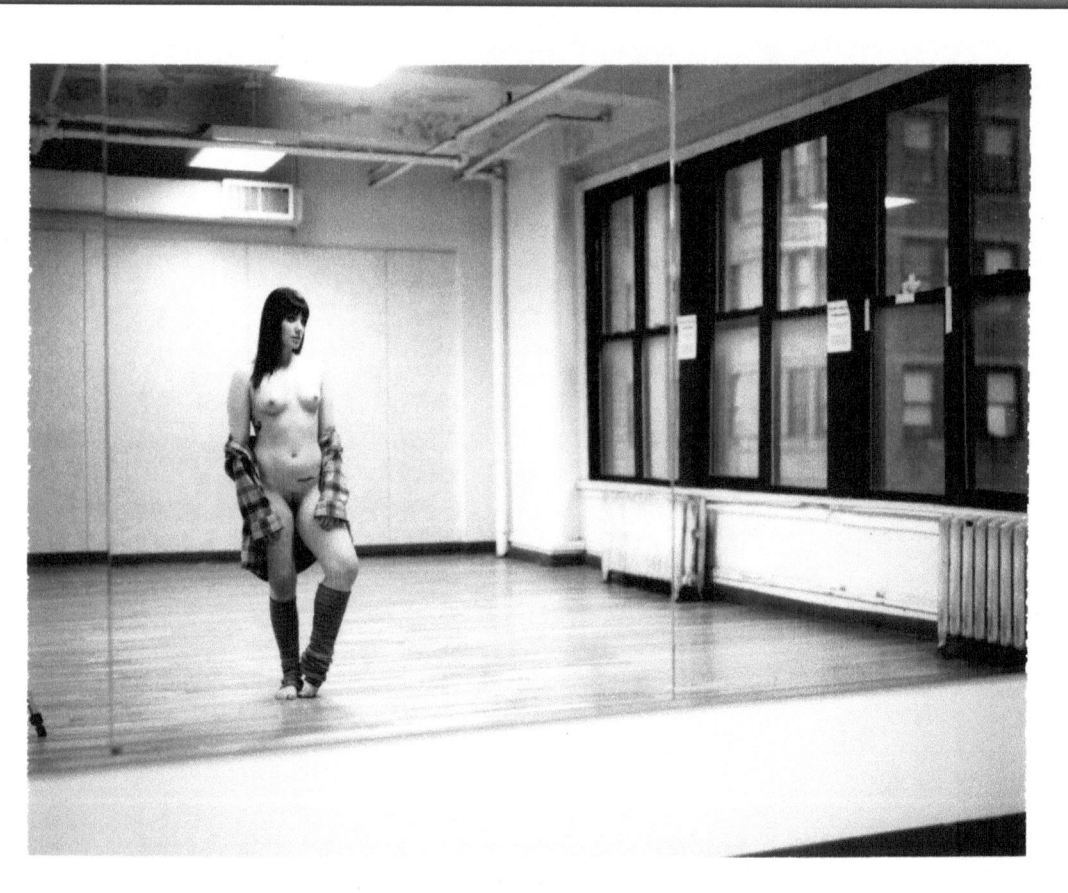

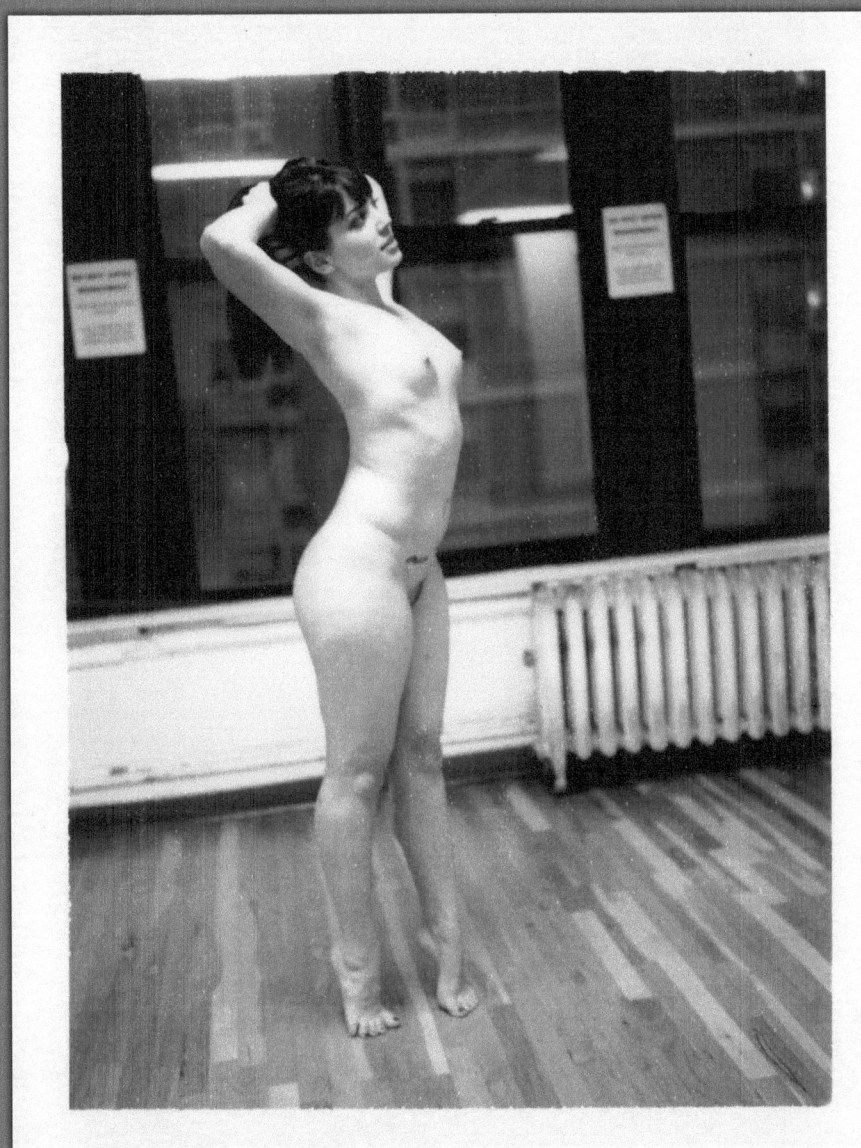

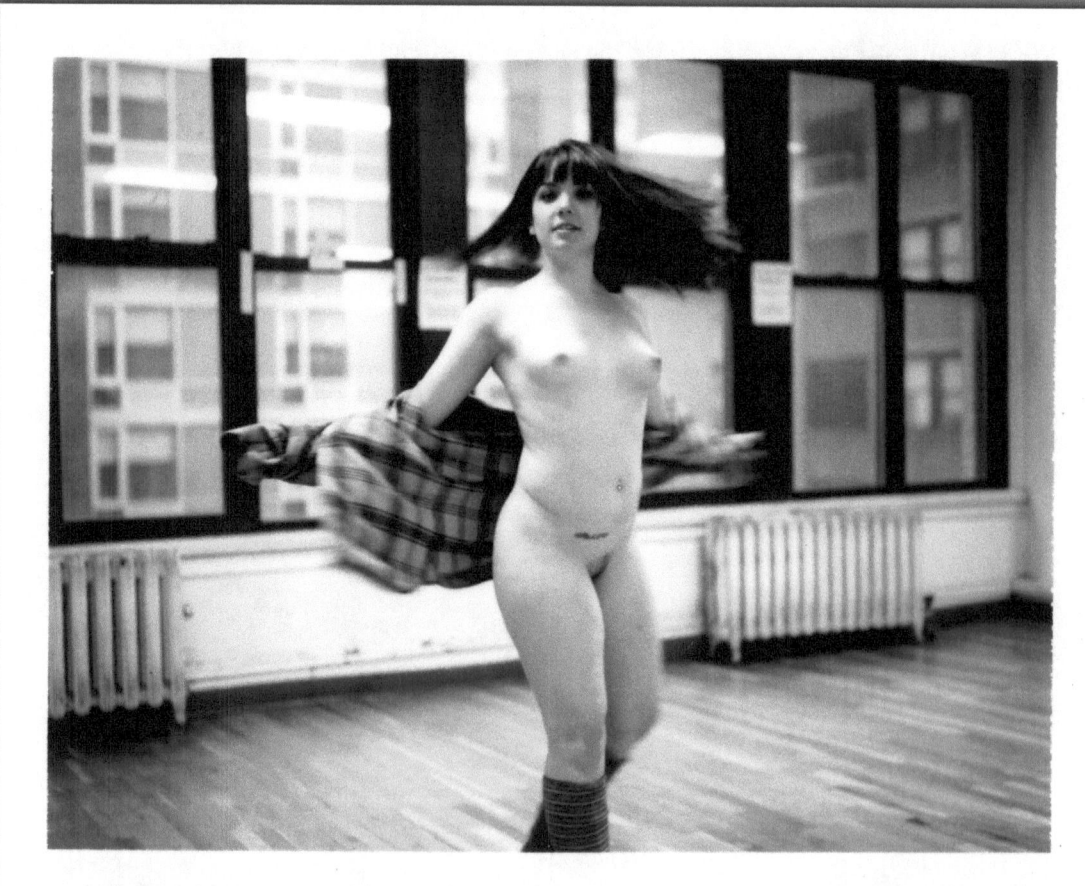

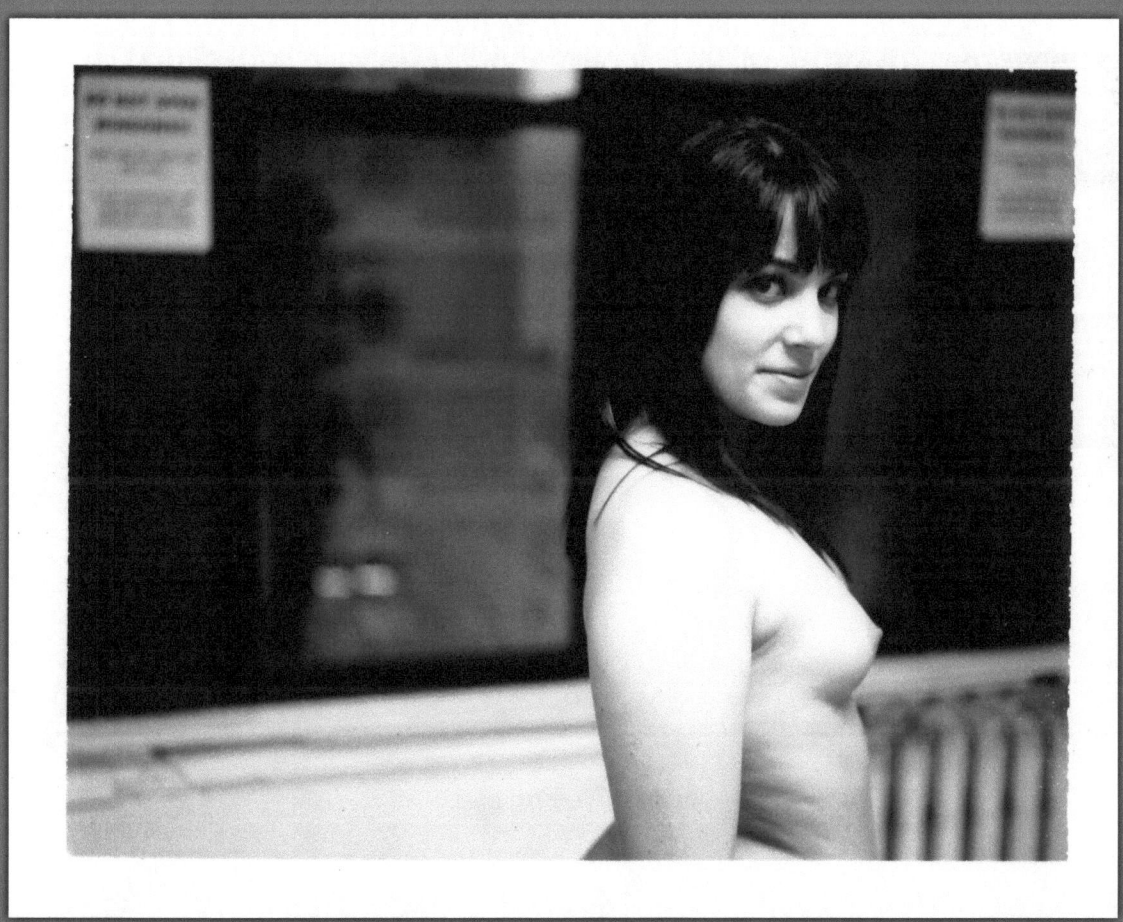

Helen

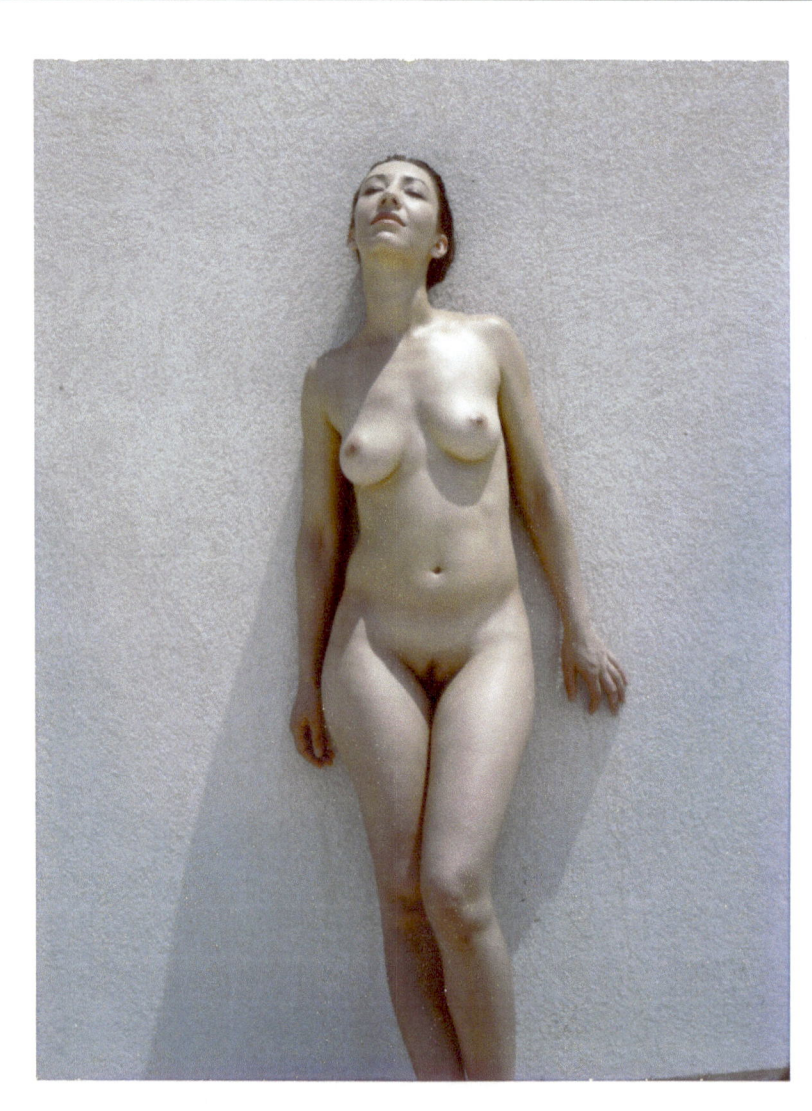

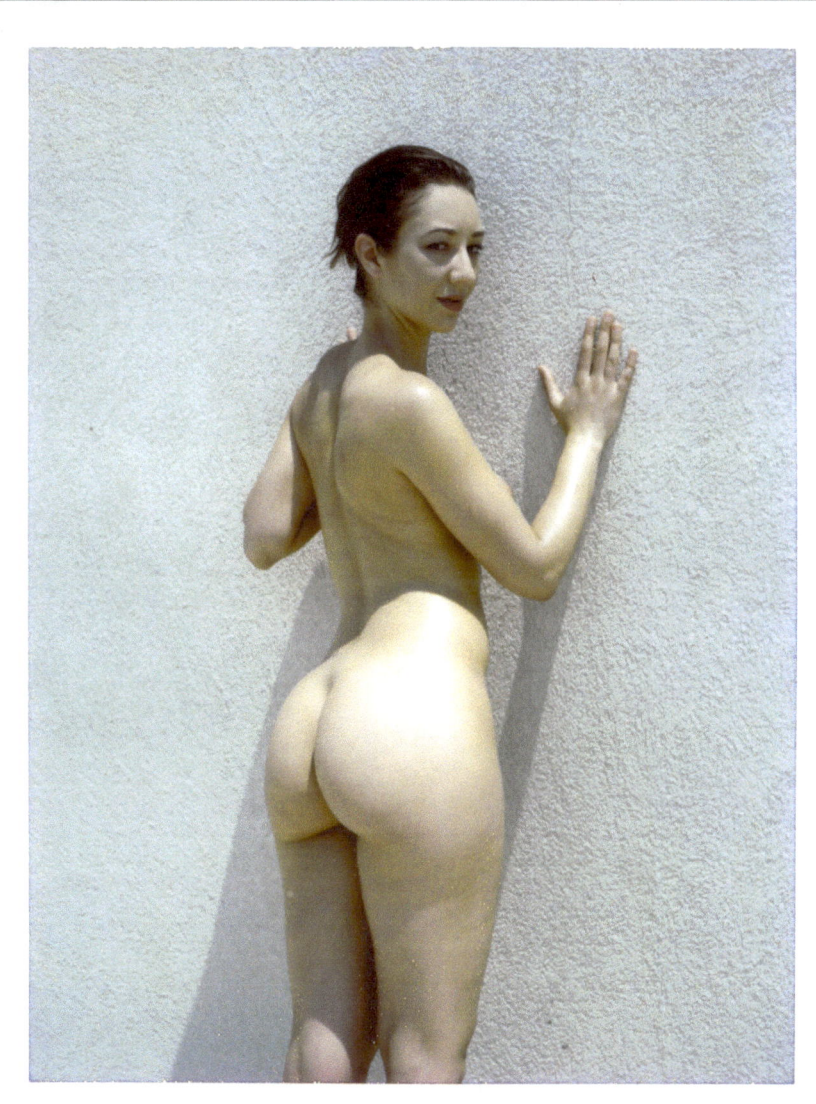

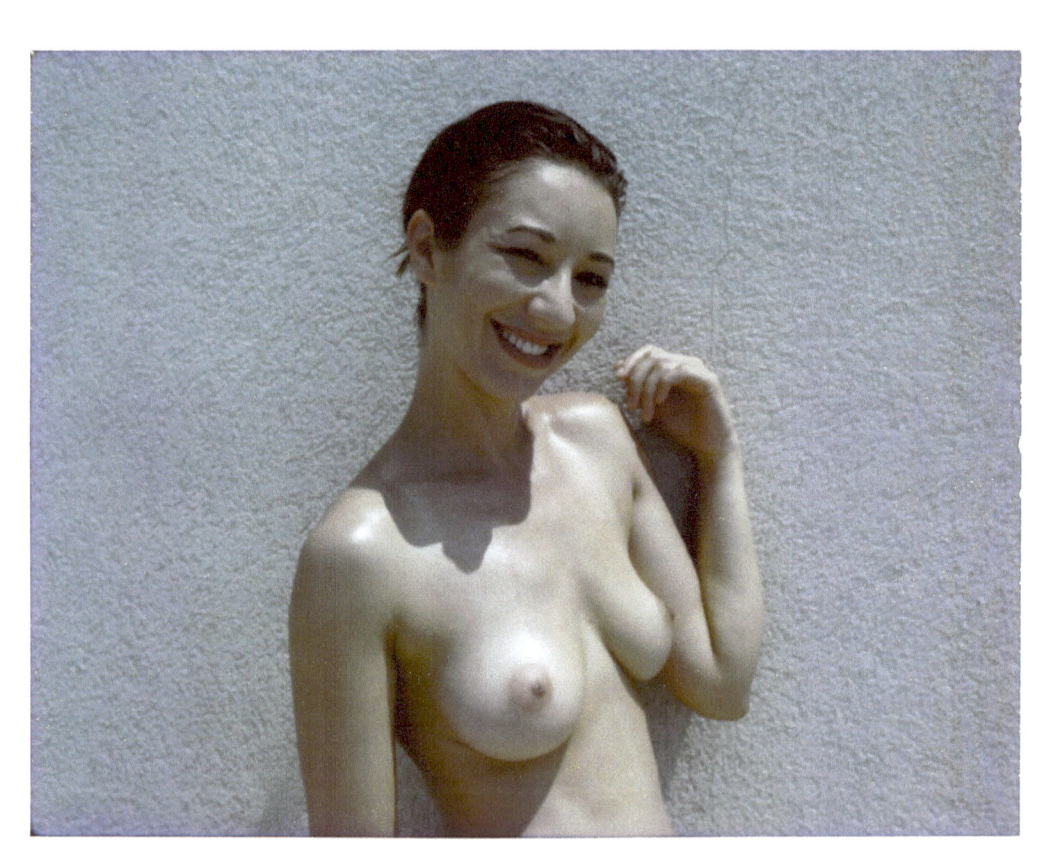

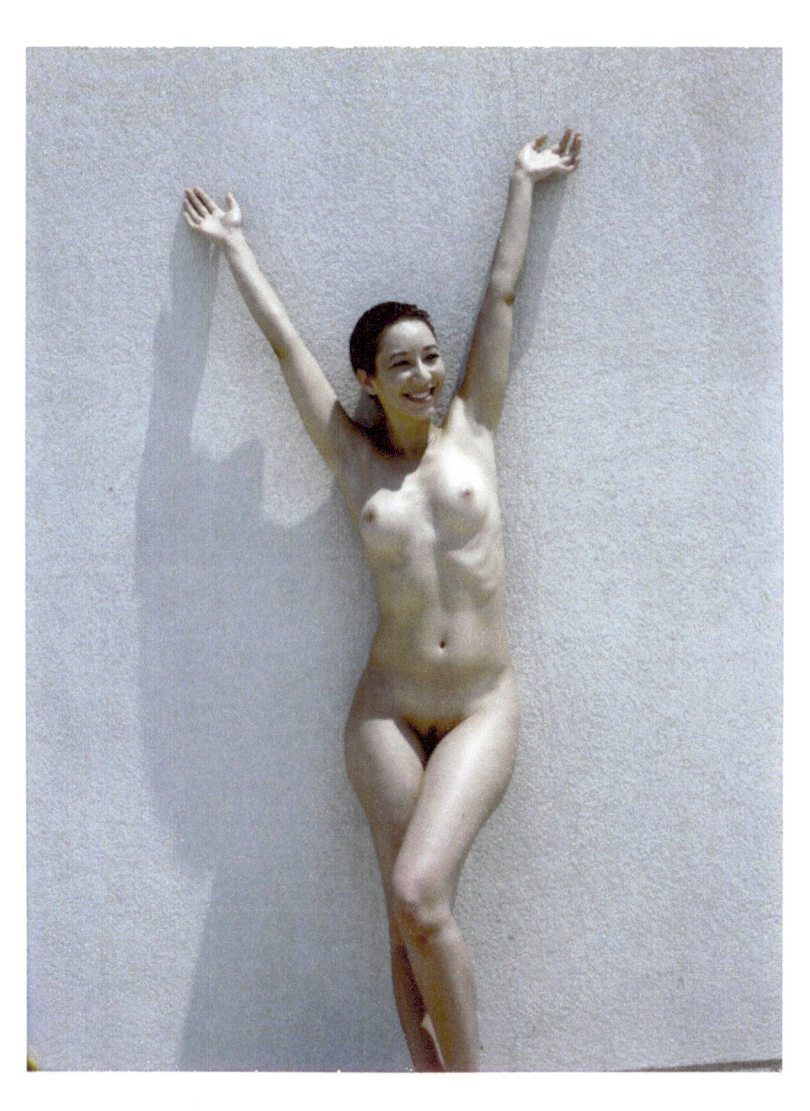

Gina

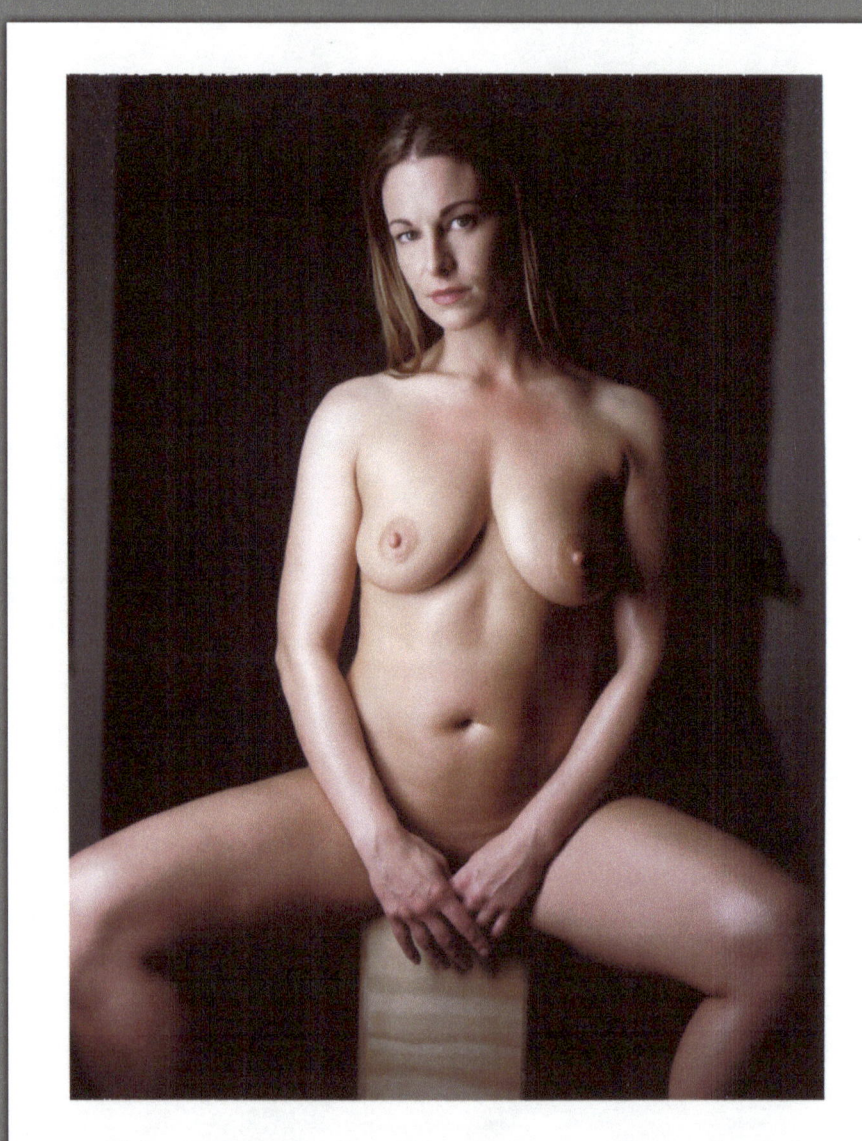

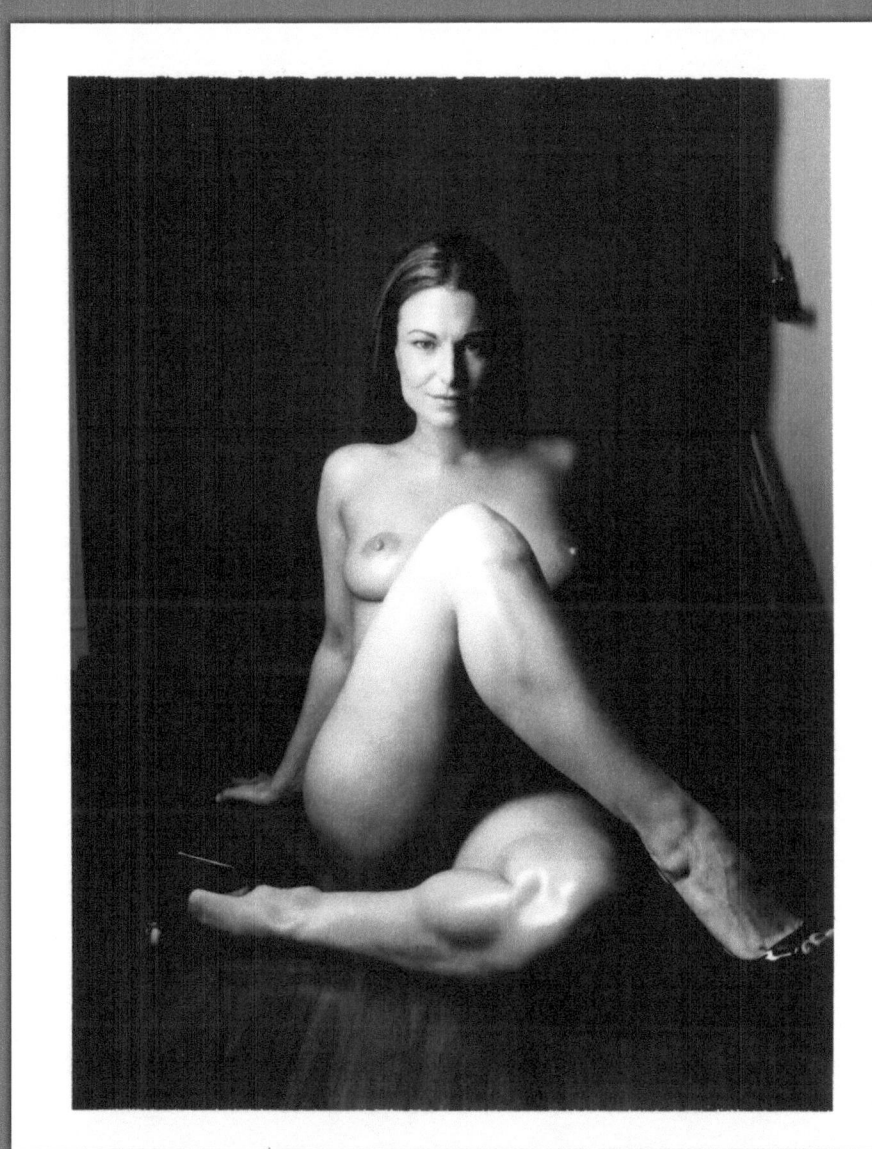

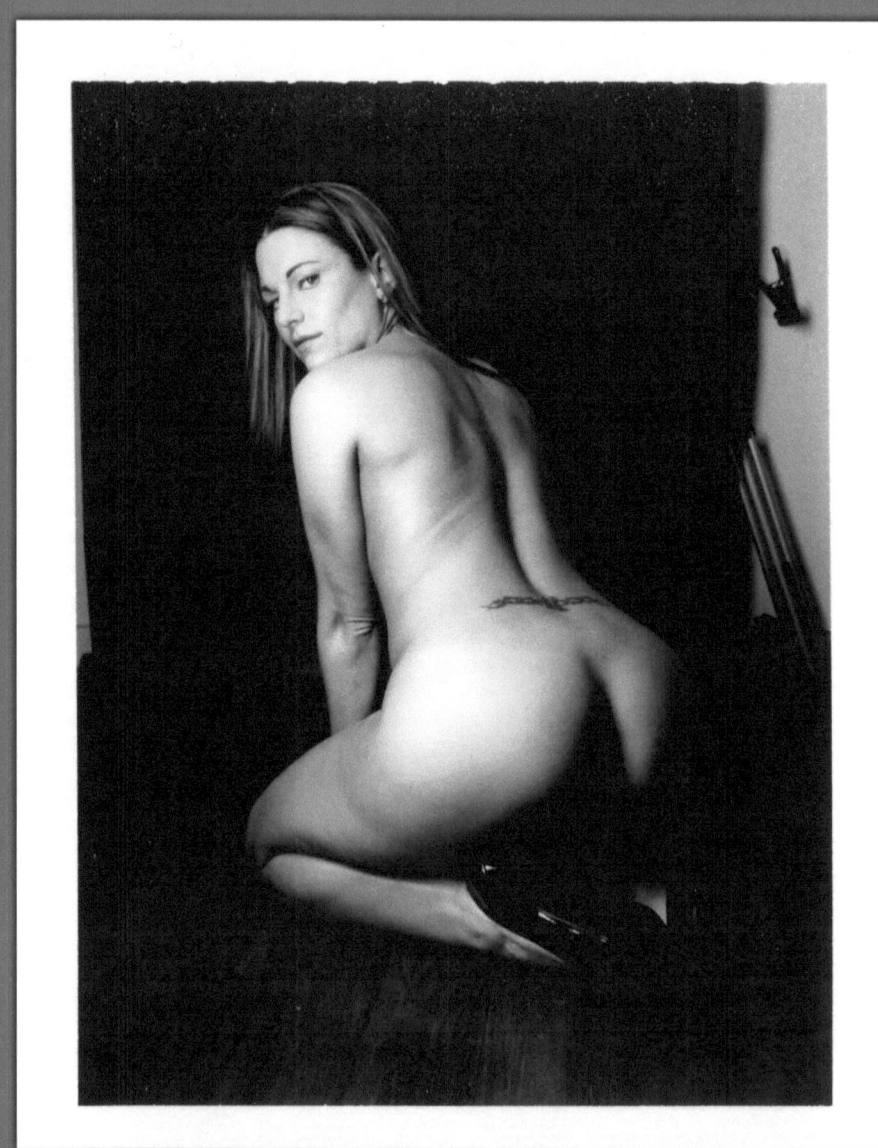

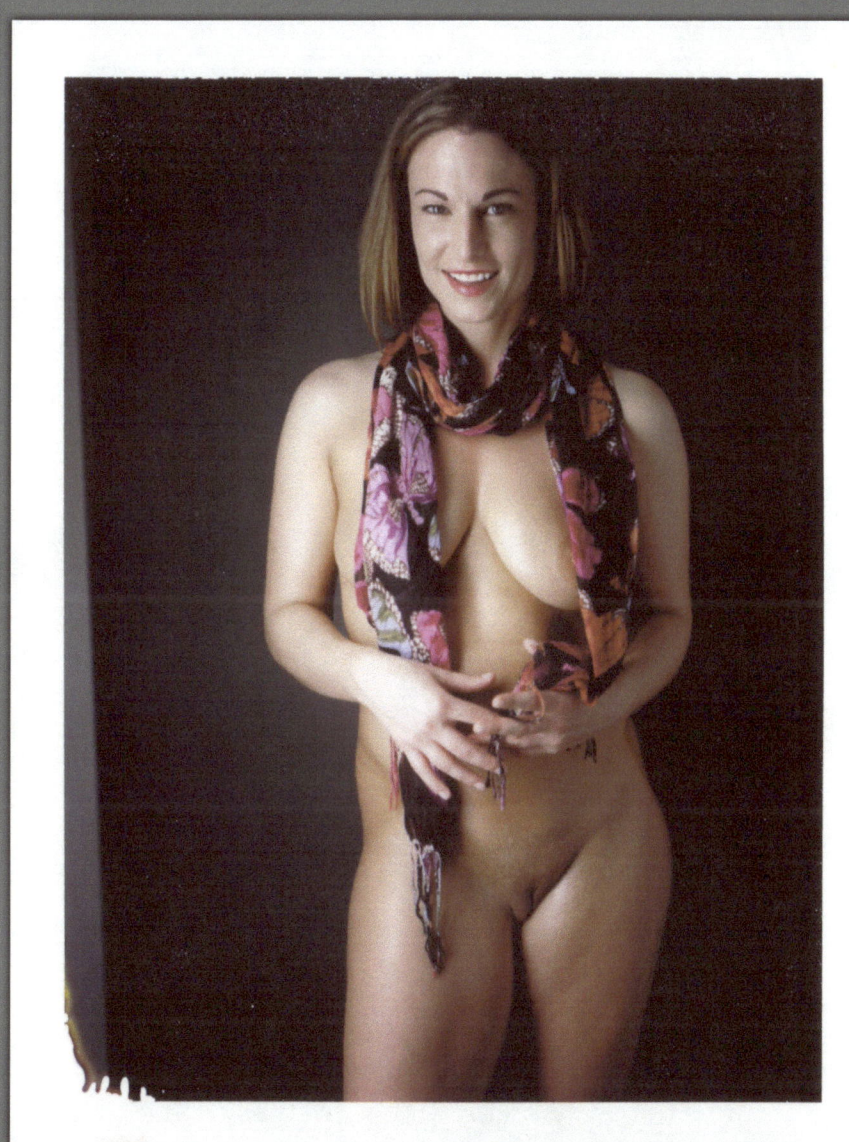

Eileen

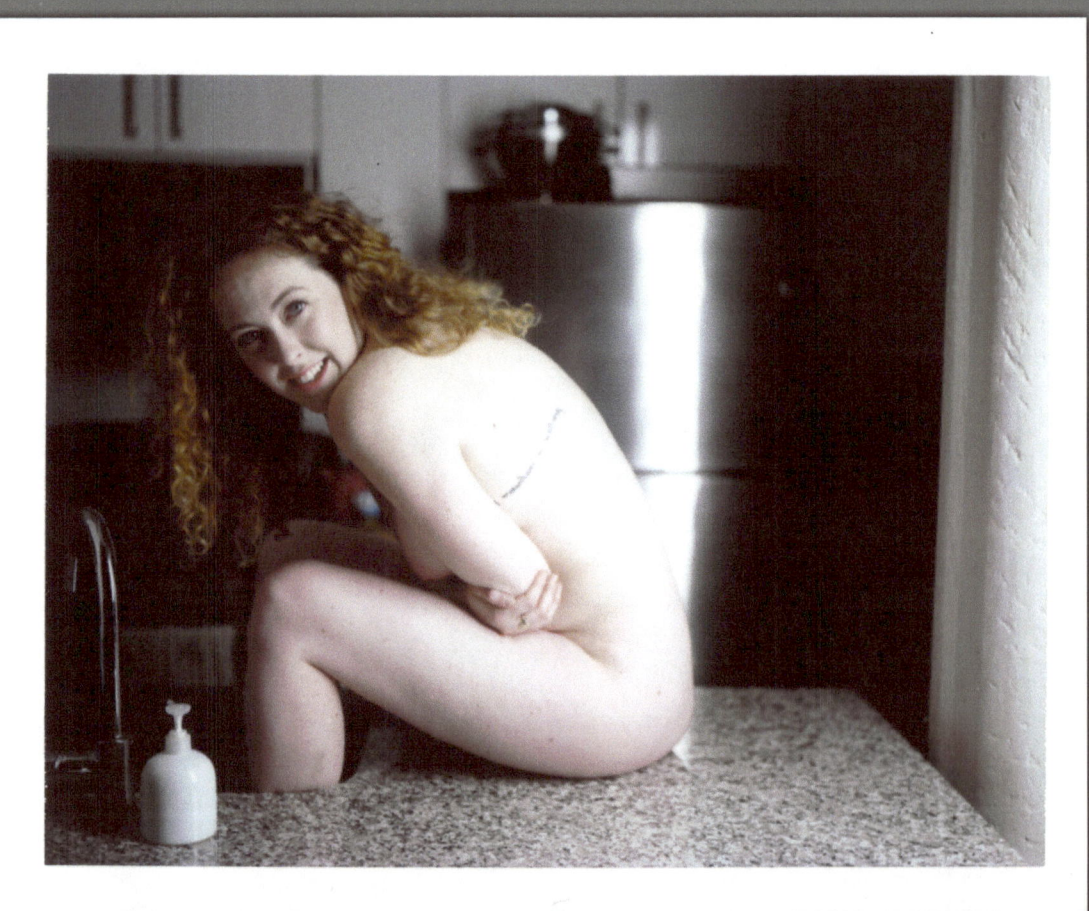

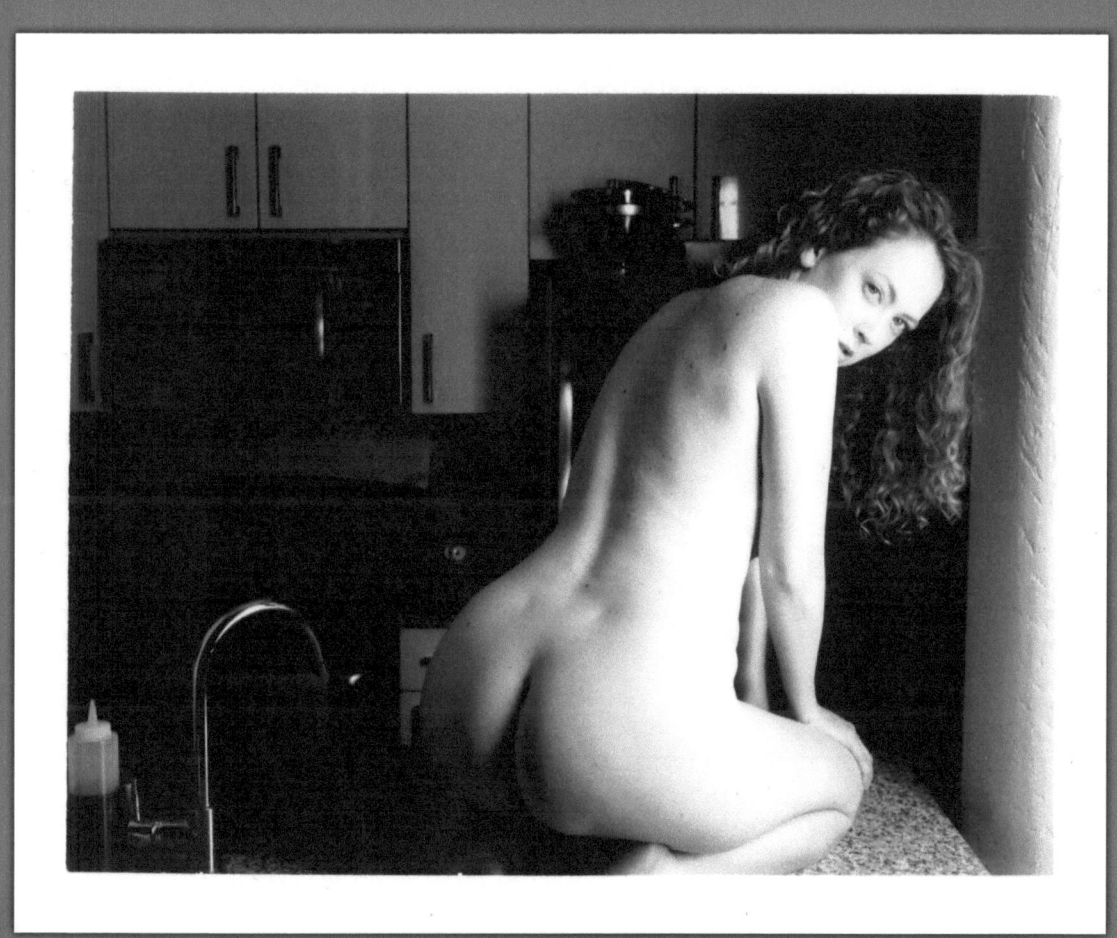

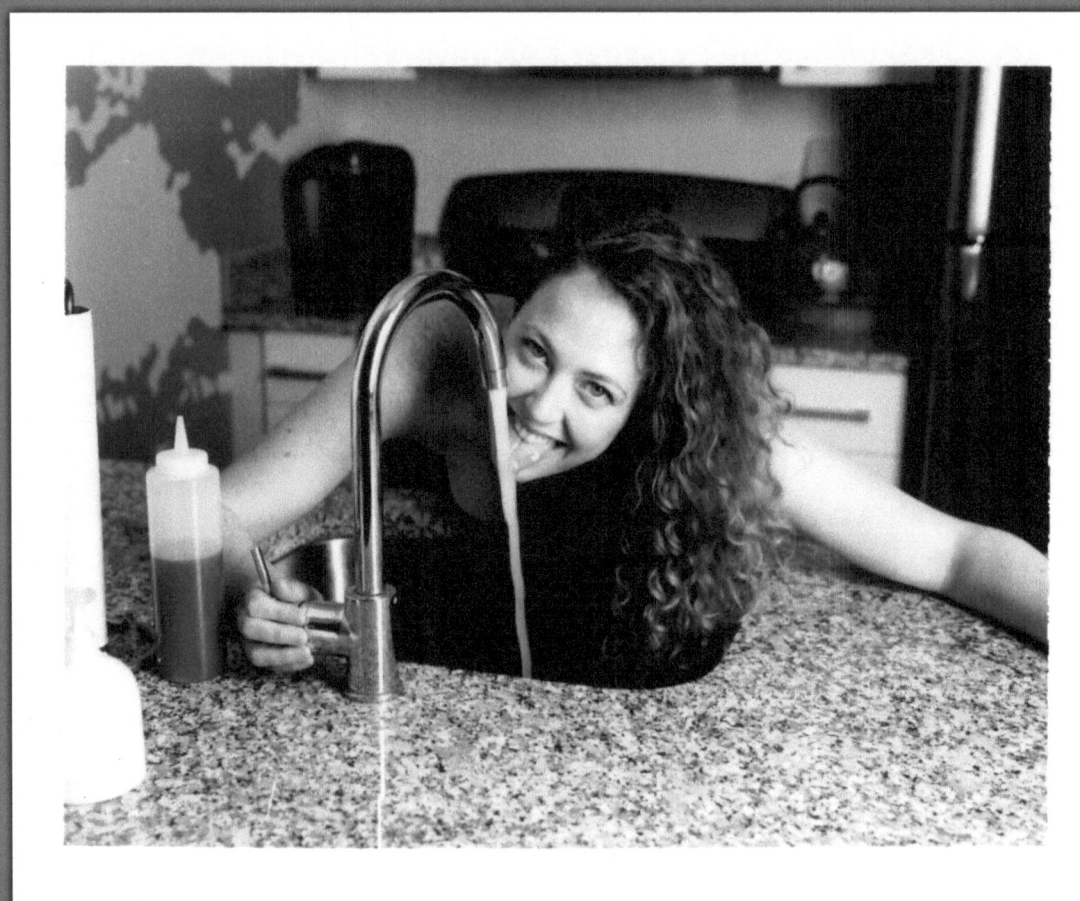

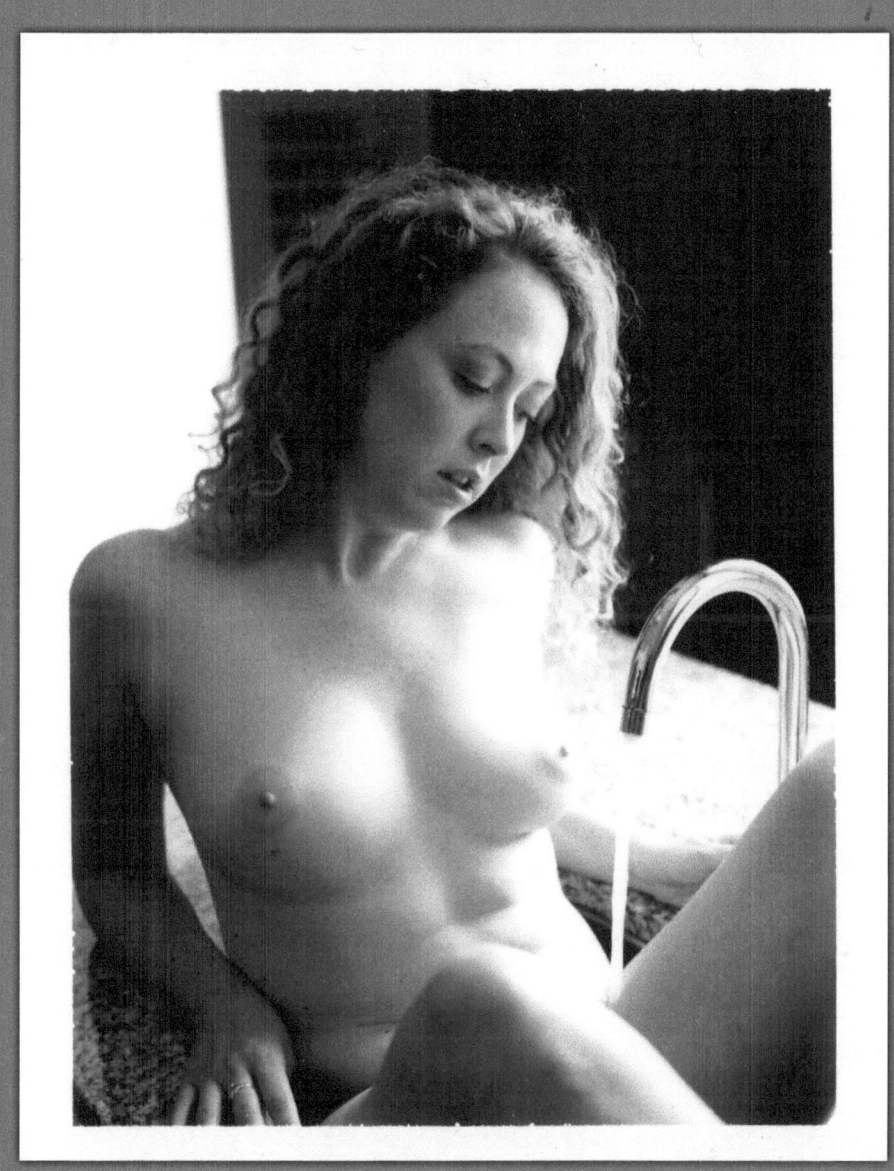

Ropo

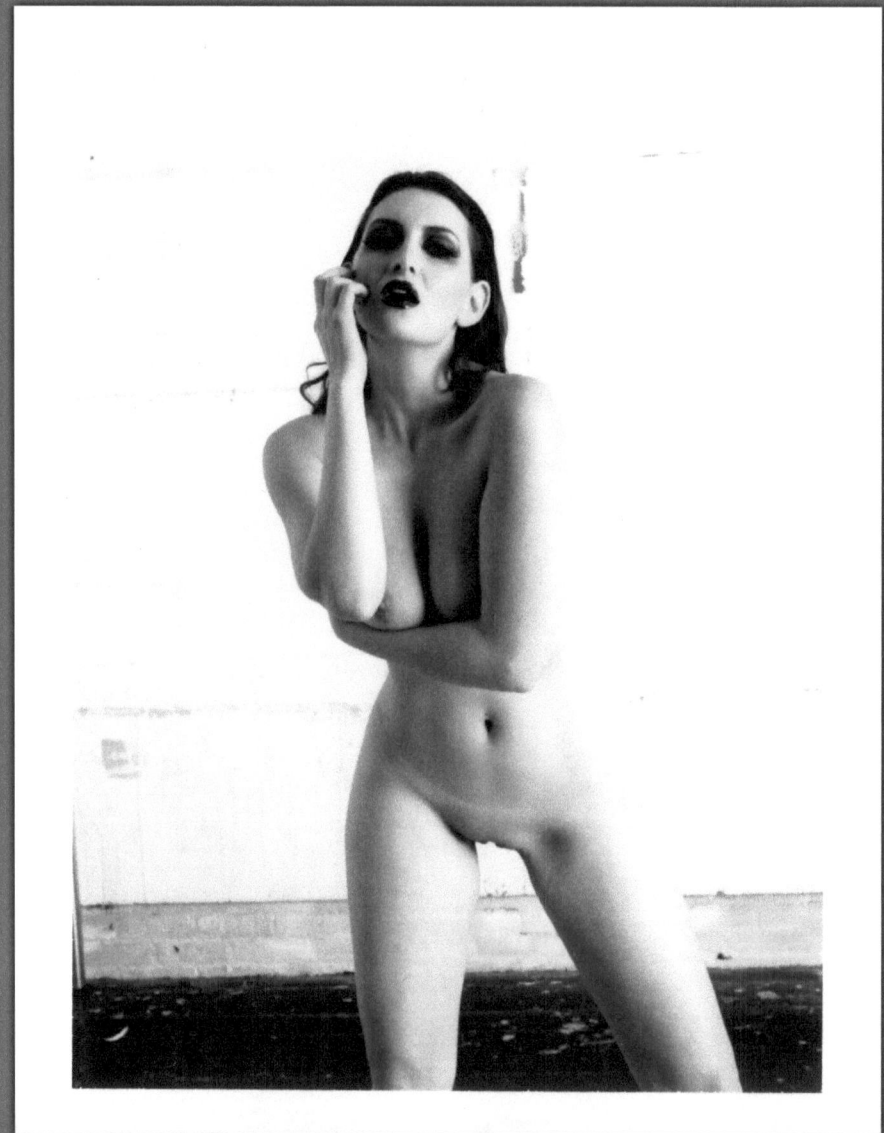

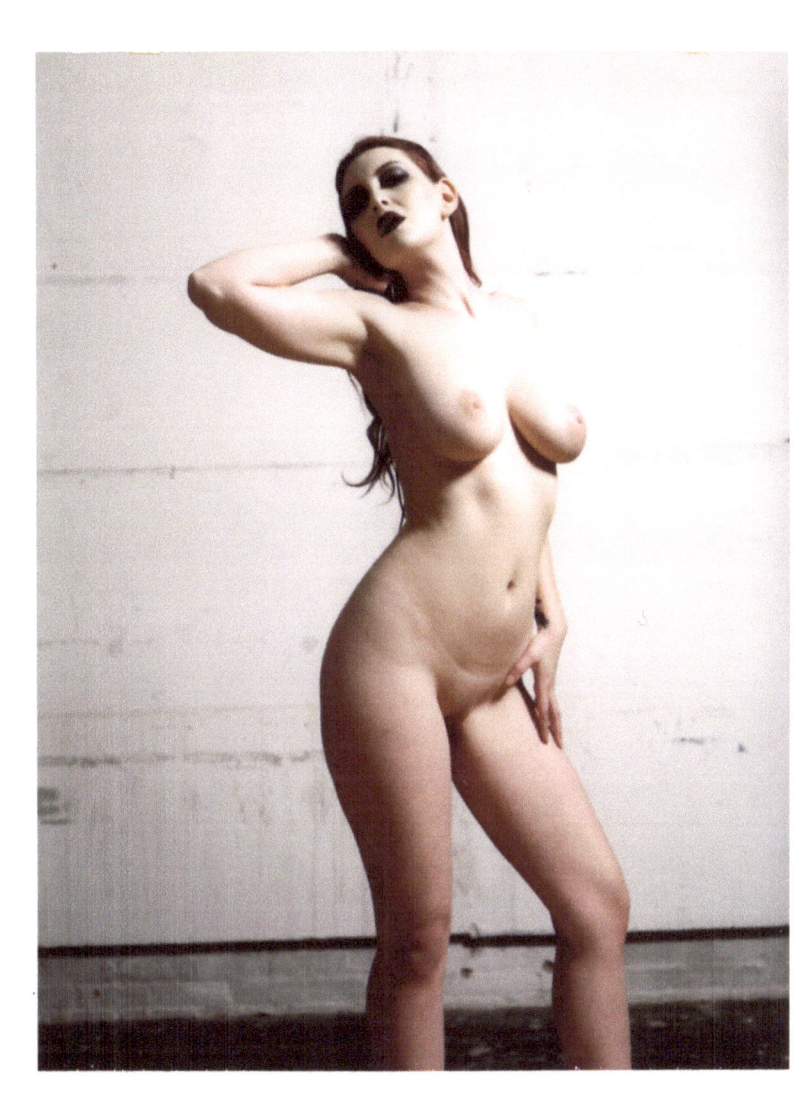

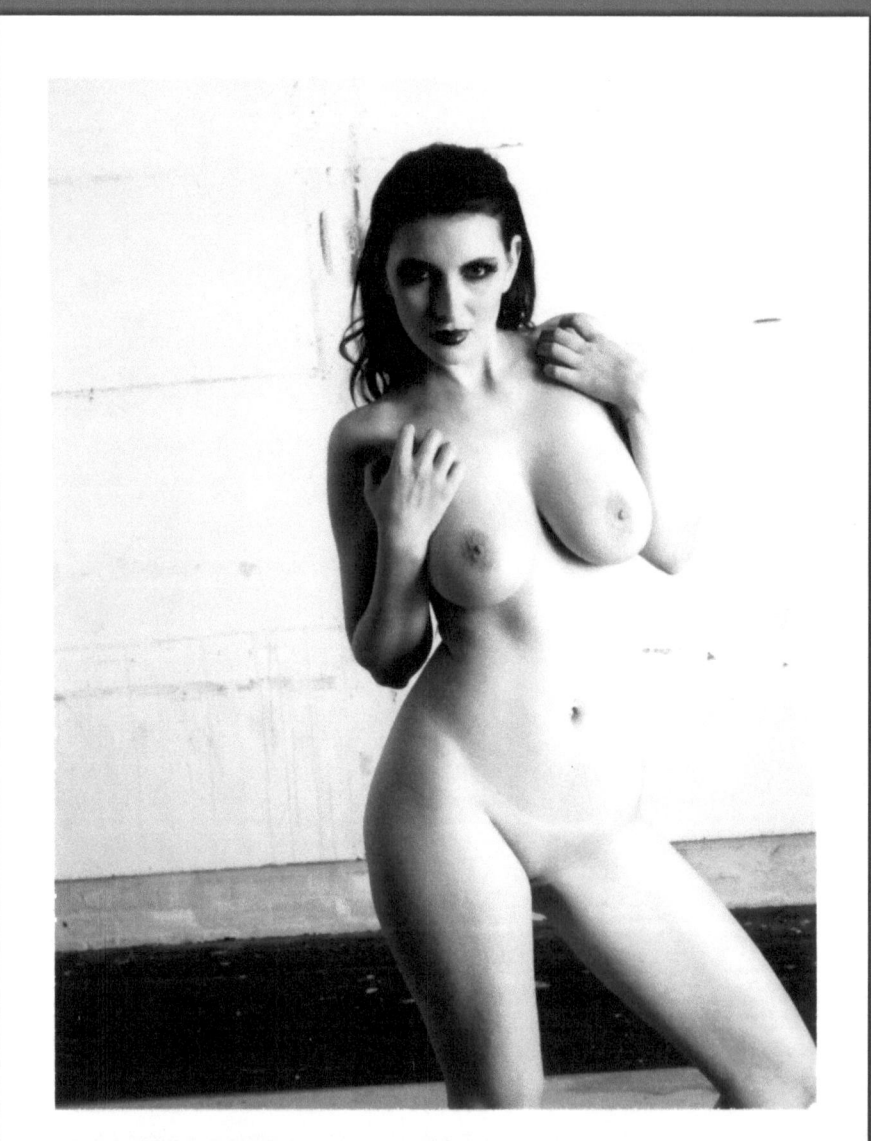

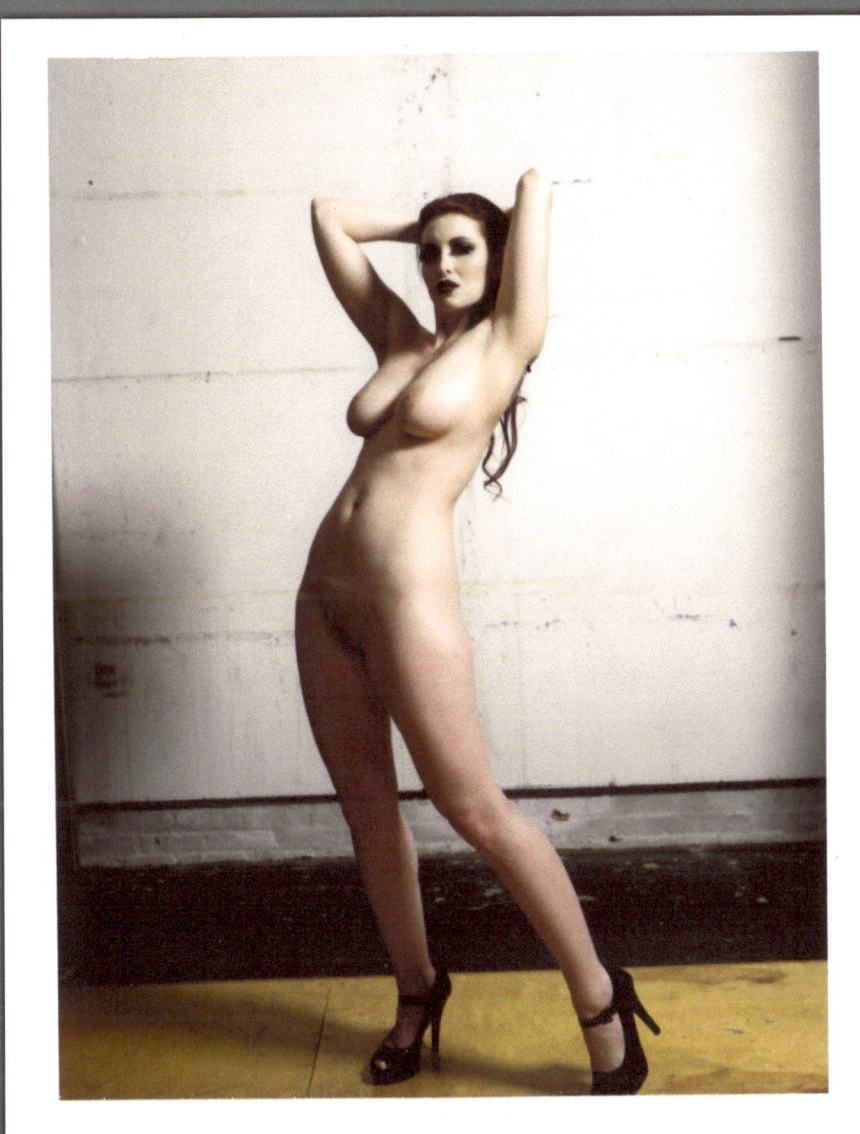

Layne

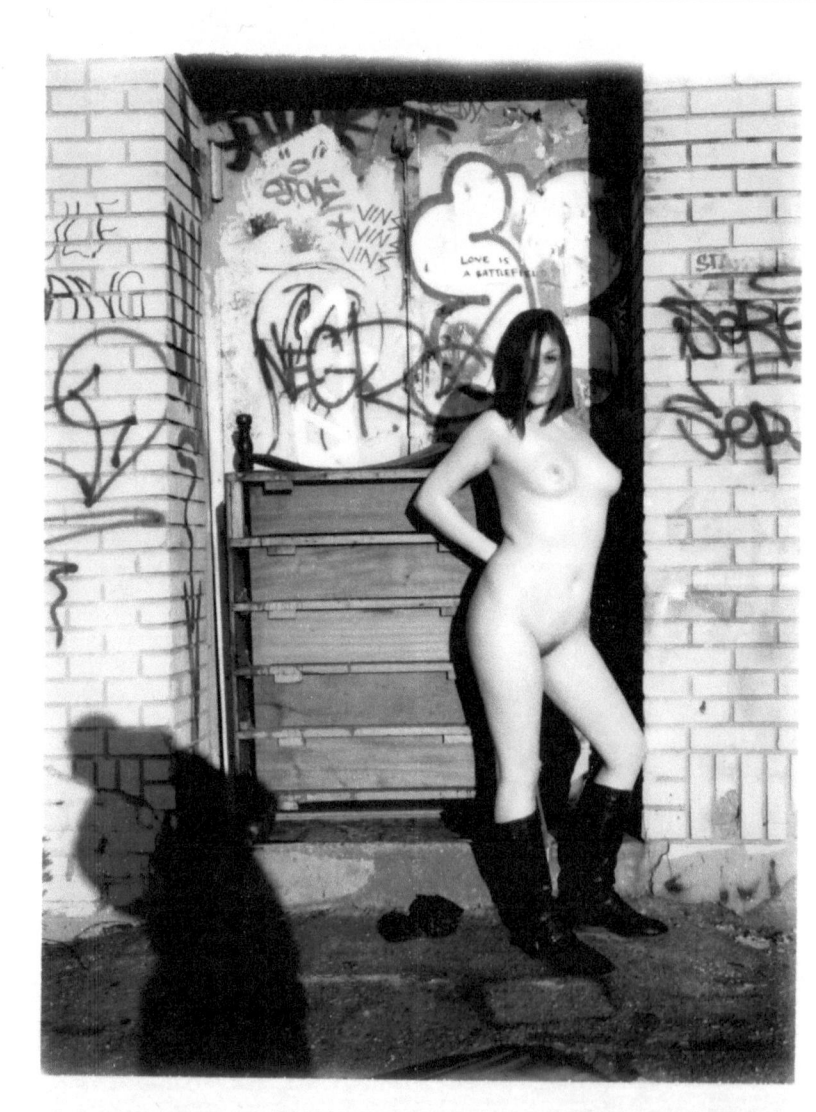

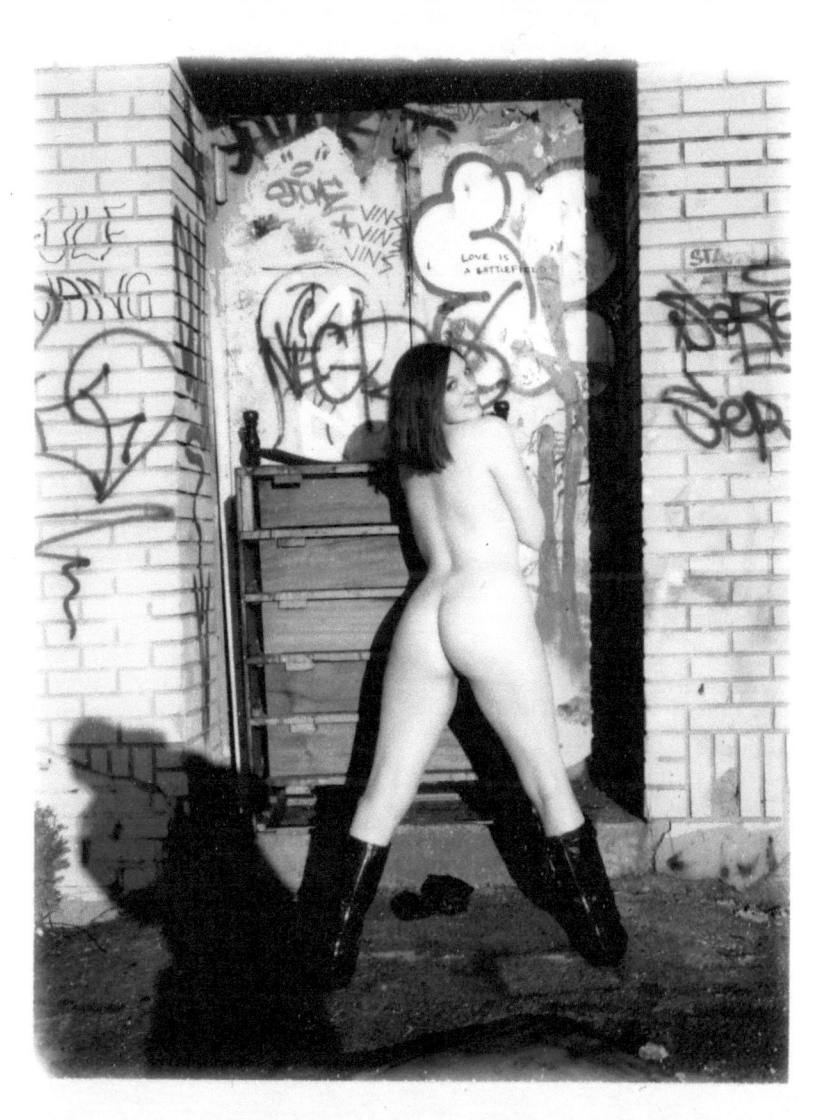

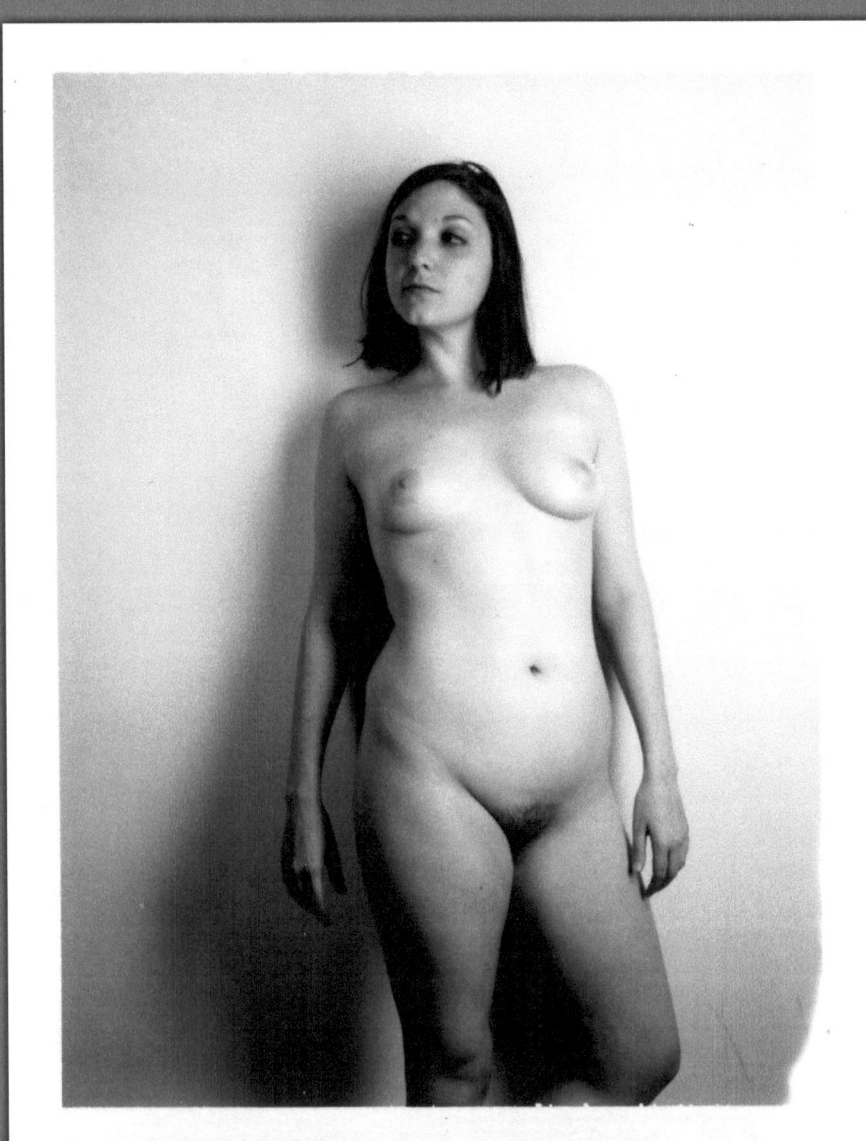

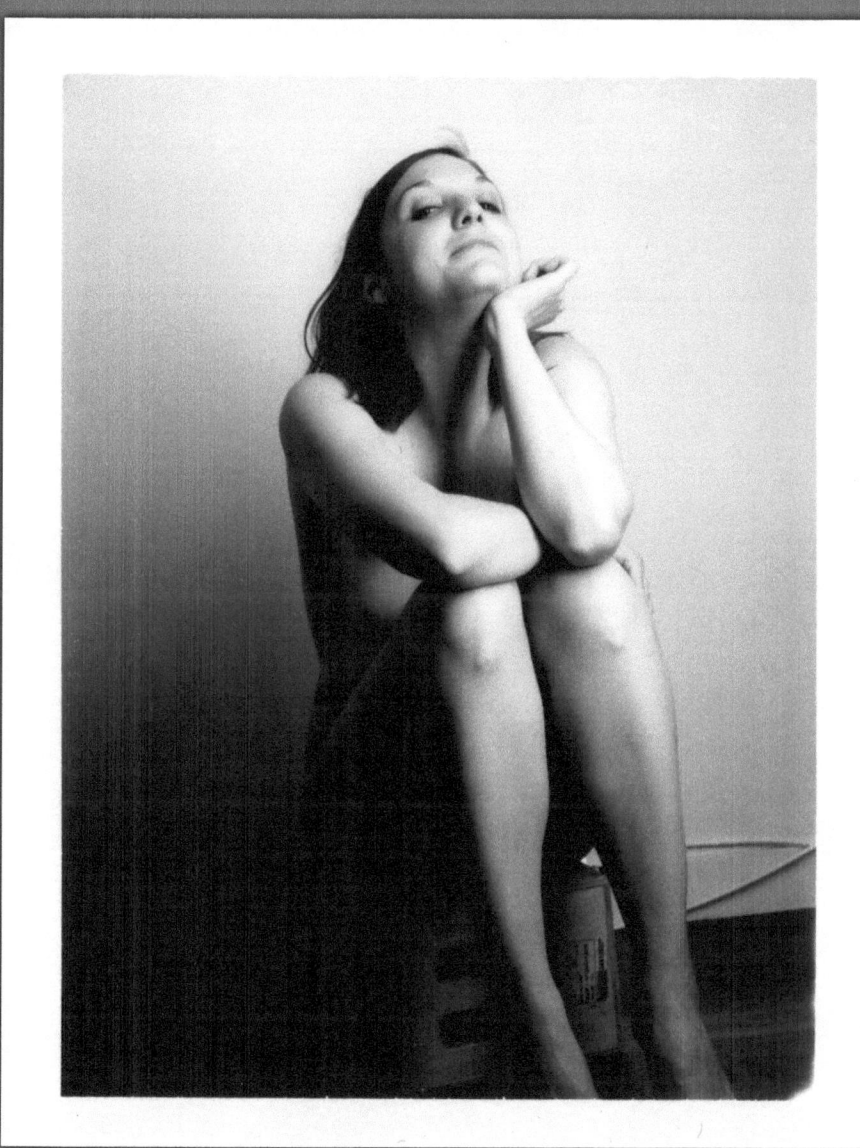

Sophie

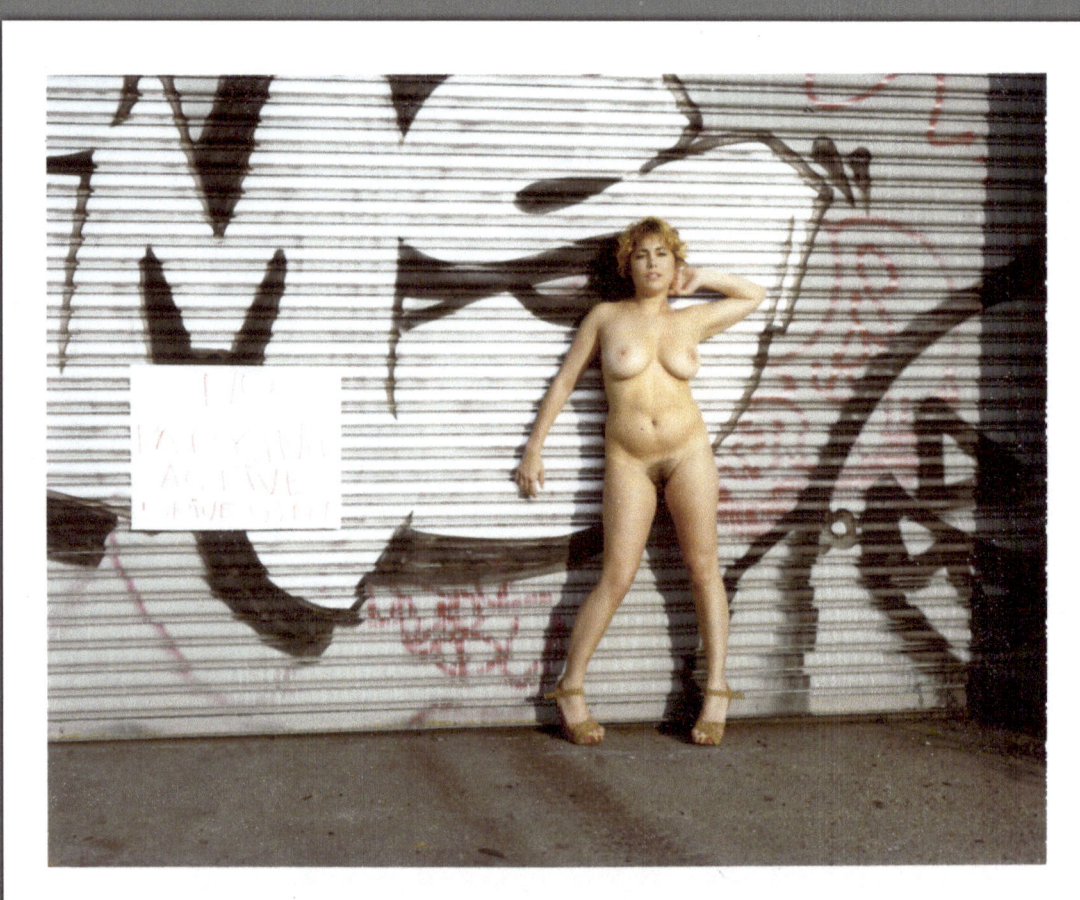

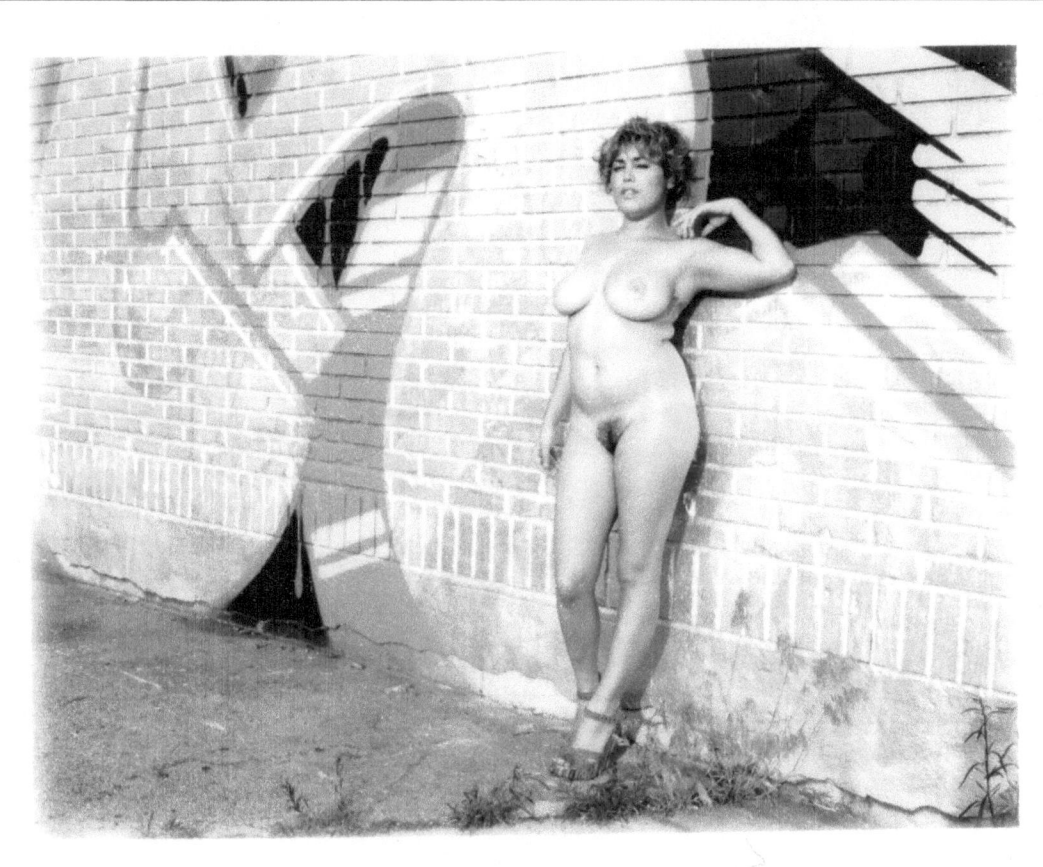

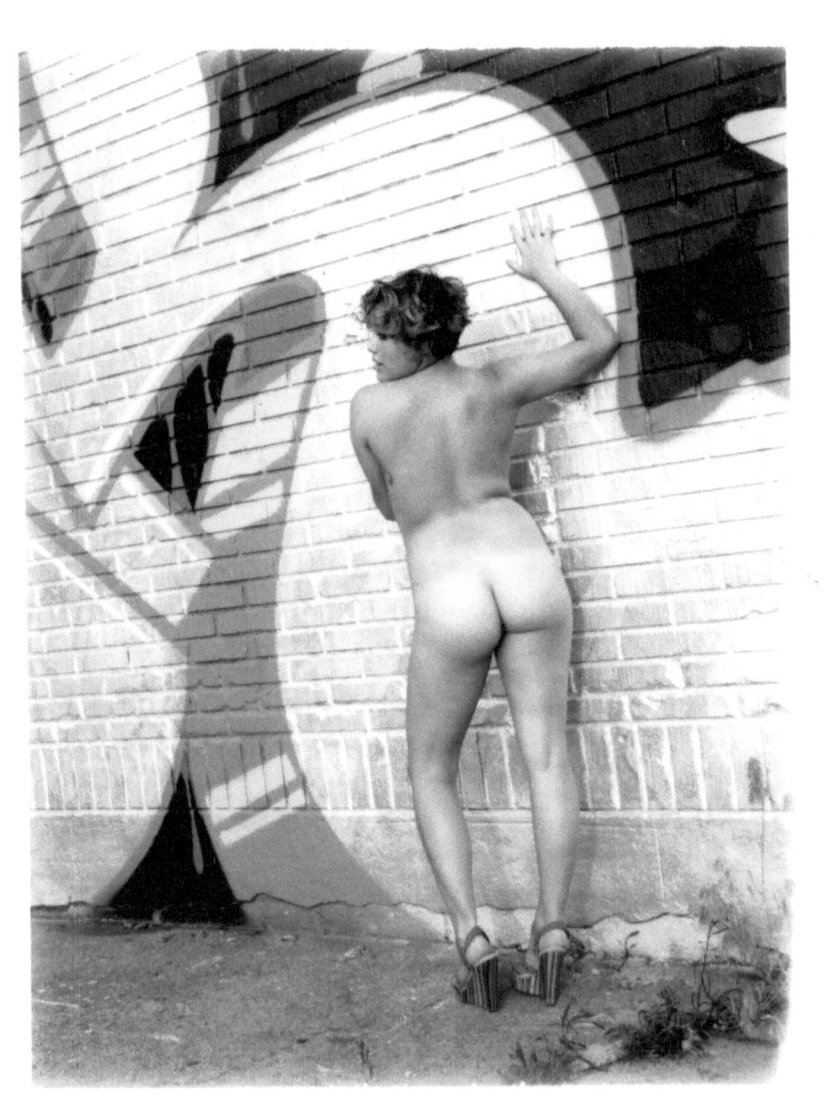

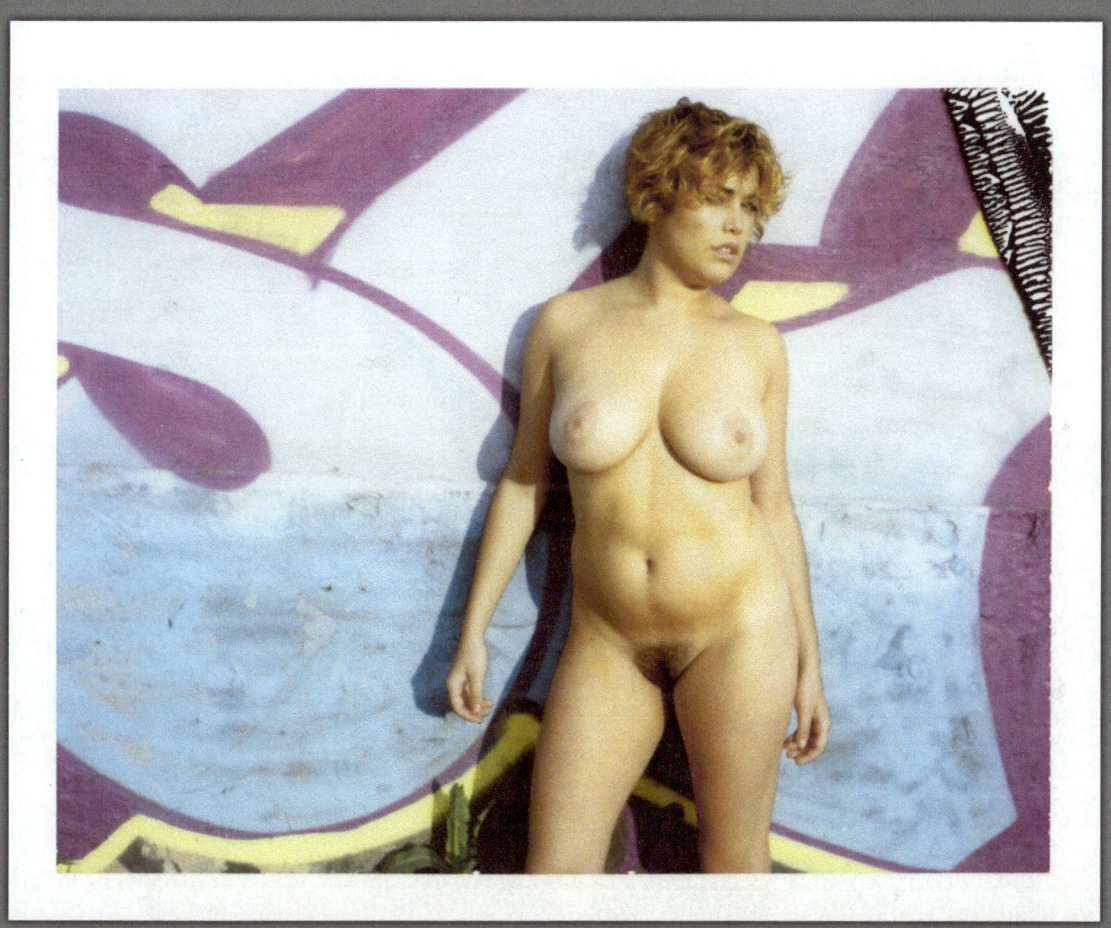

Rachel

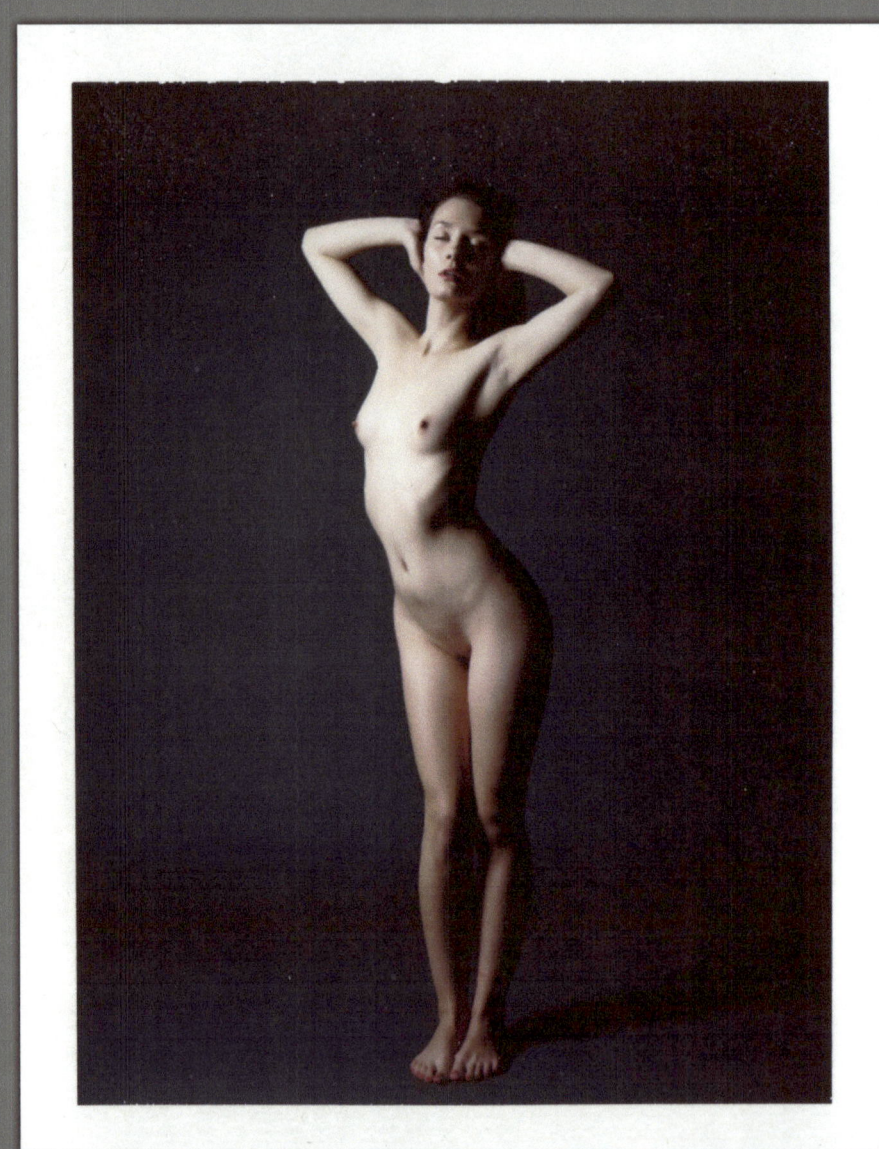

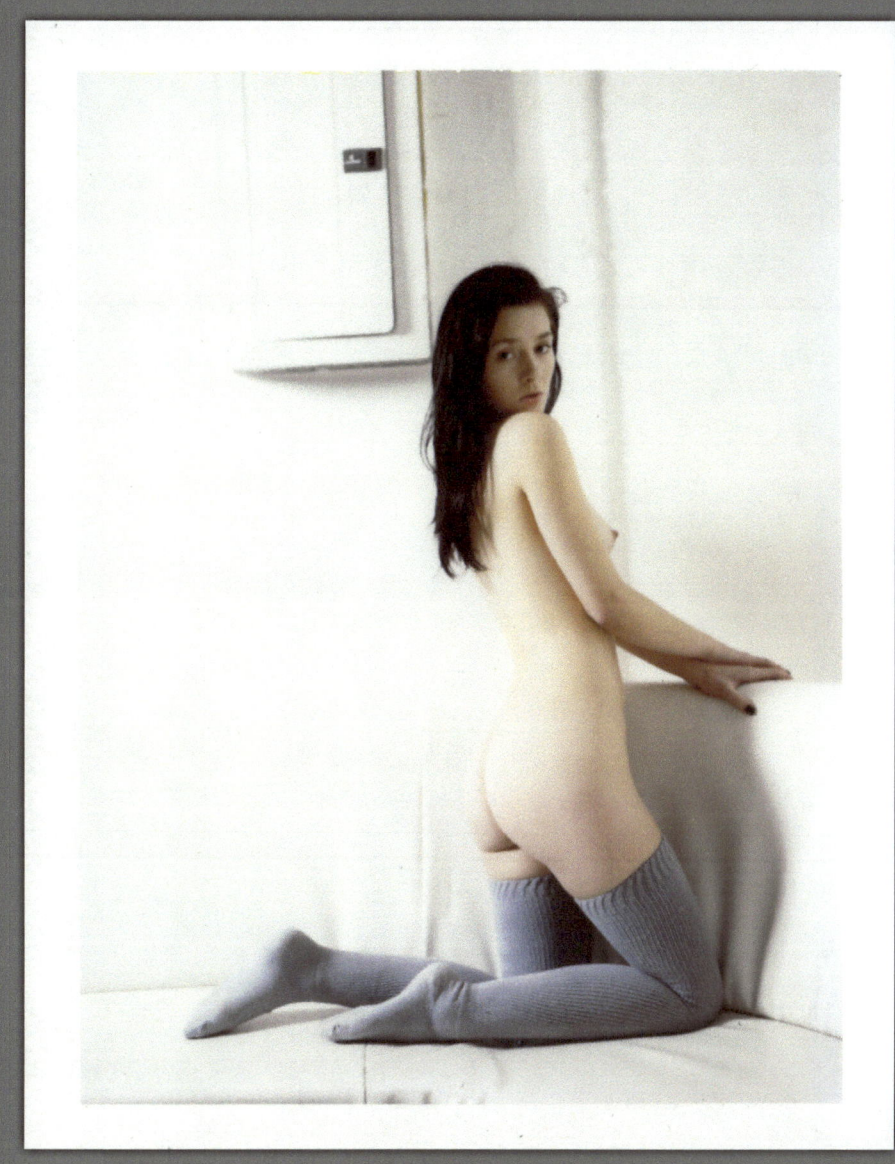

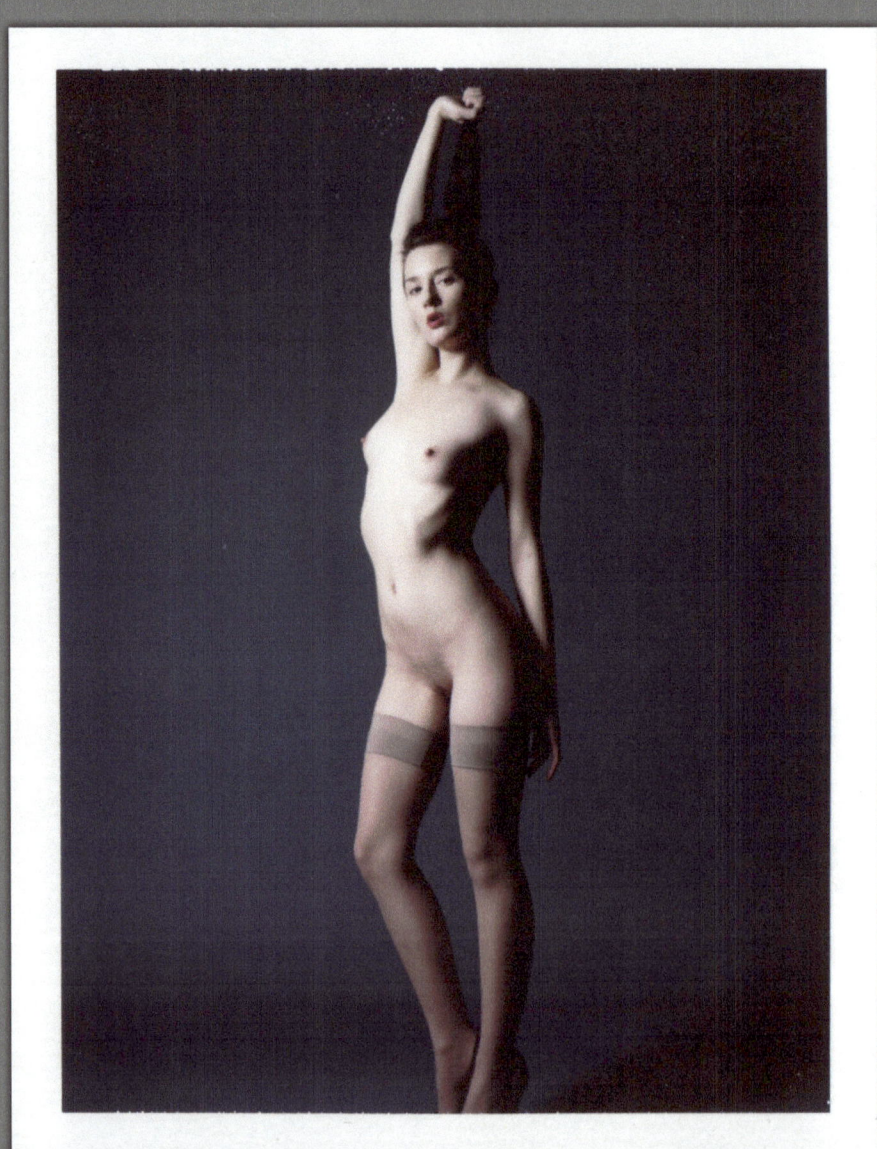

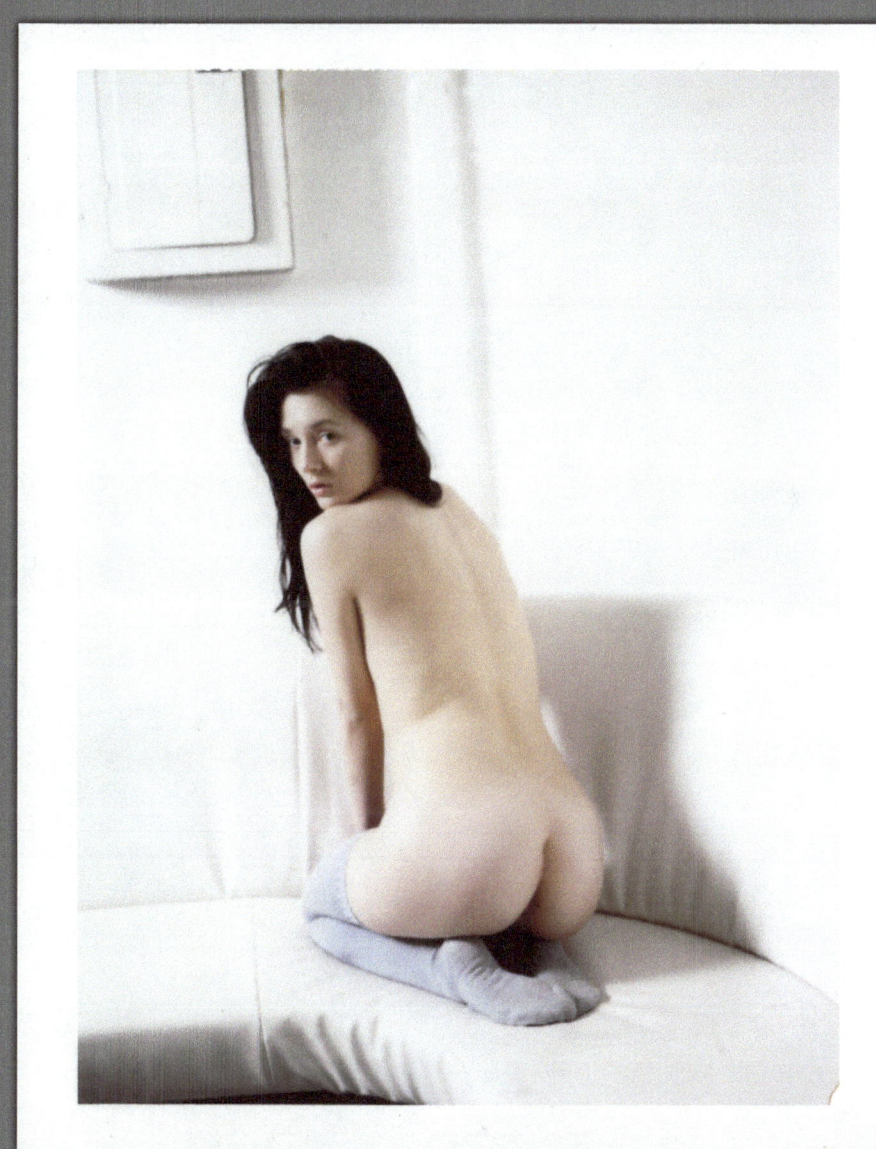

Em

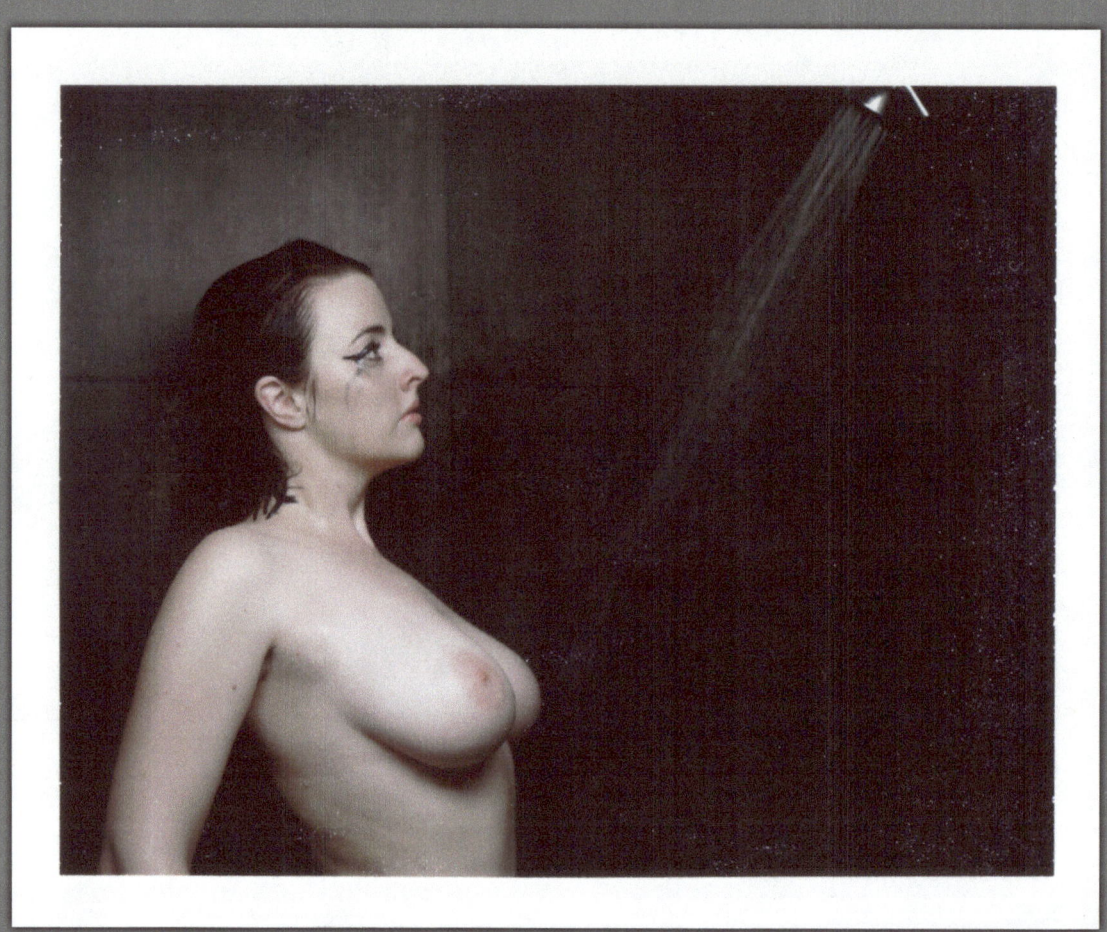

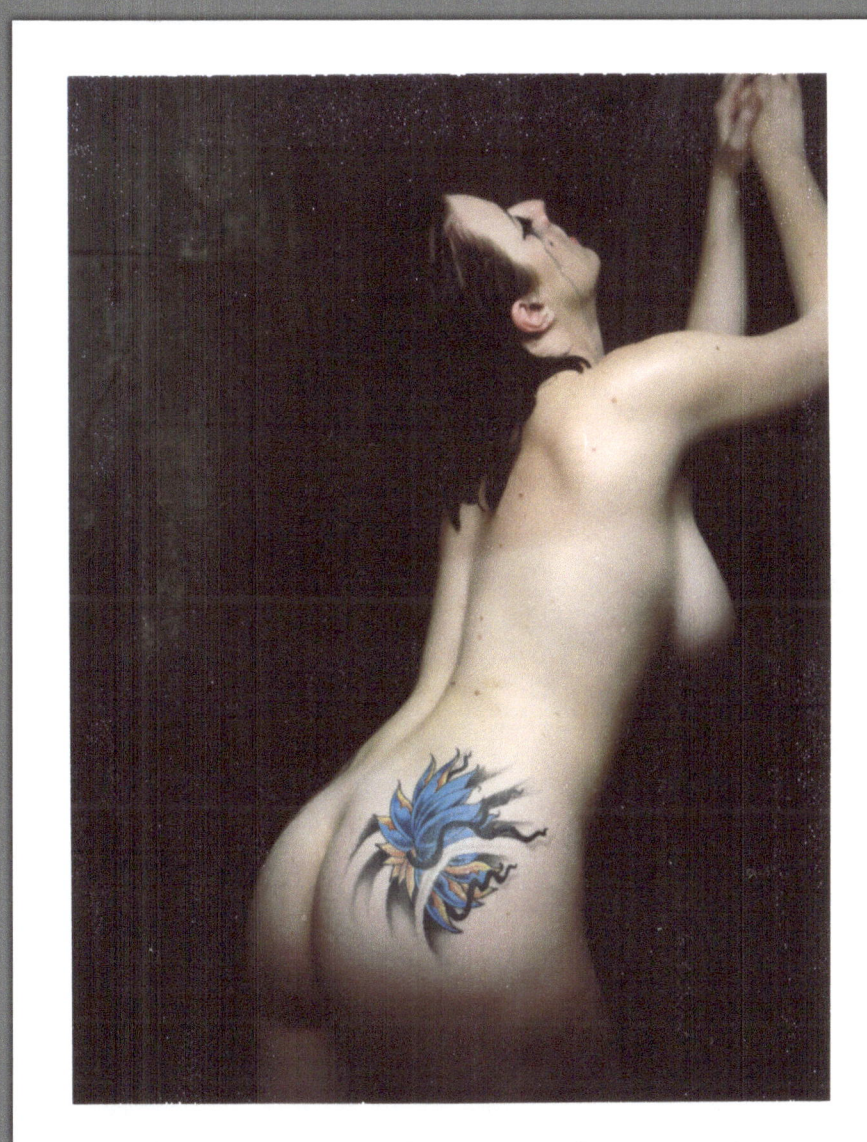

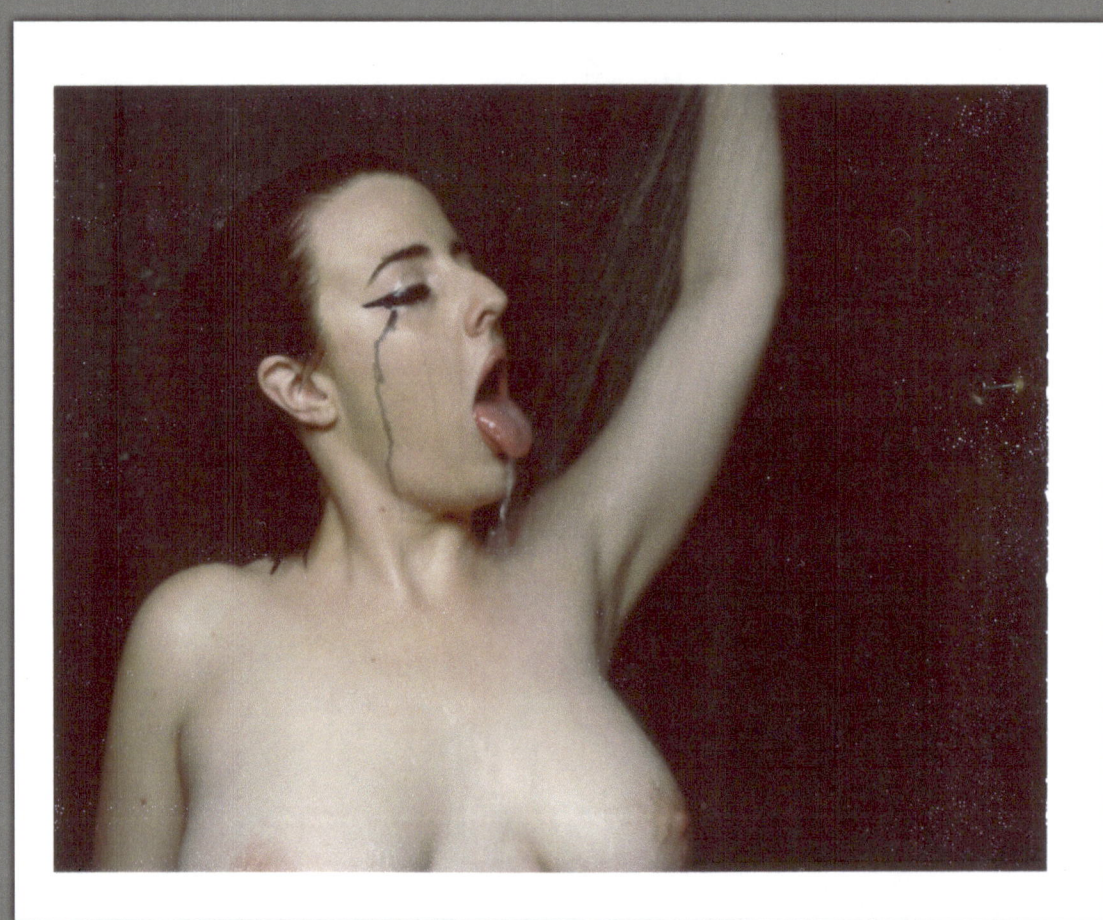

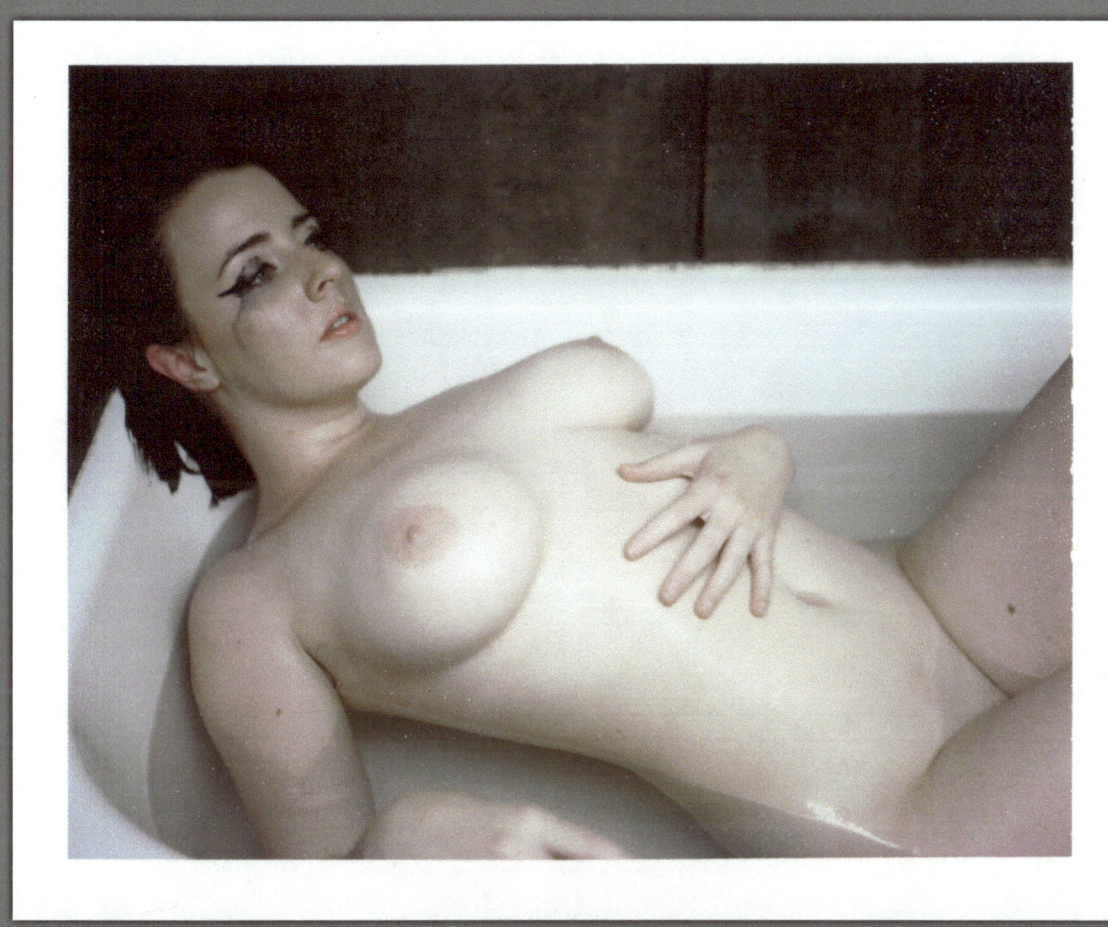

Tanya

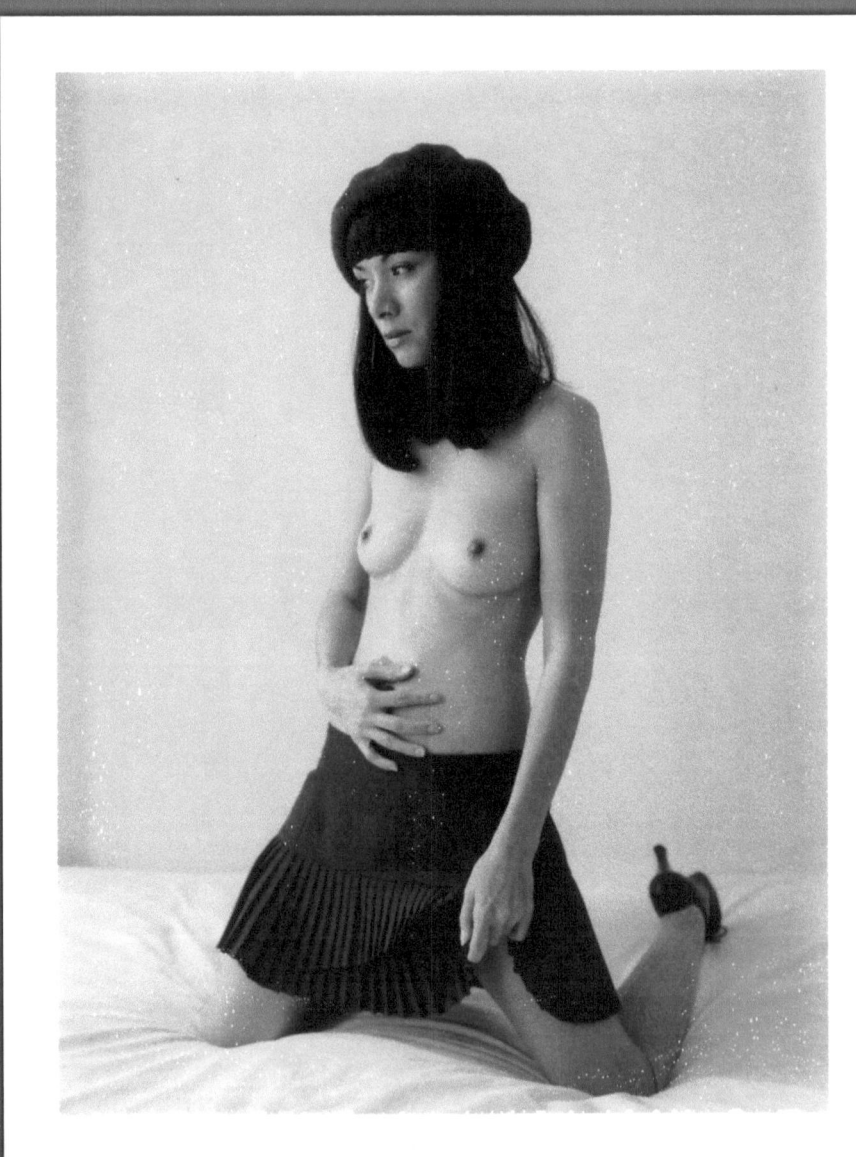

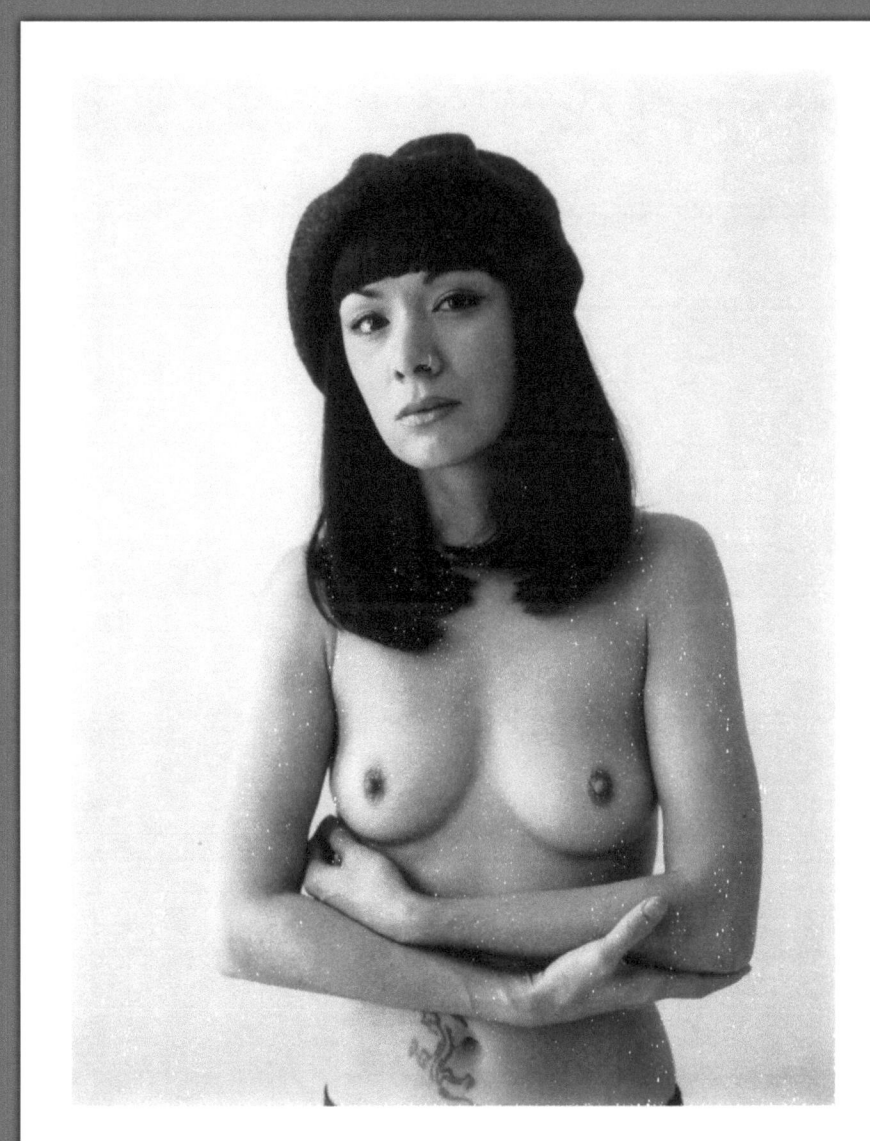

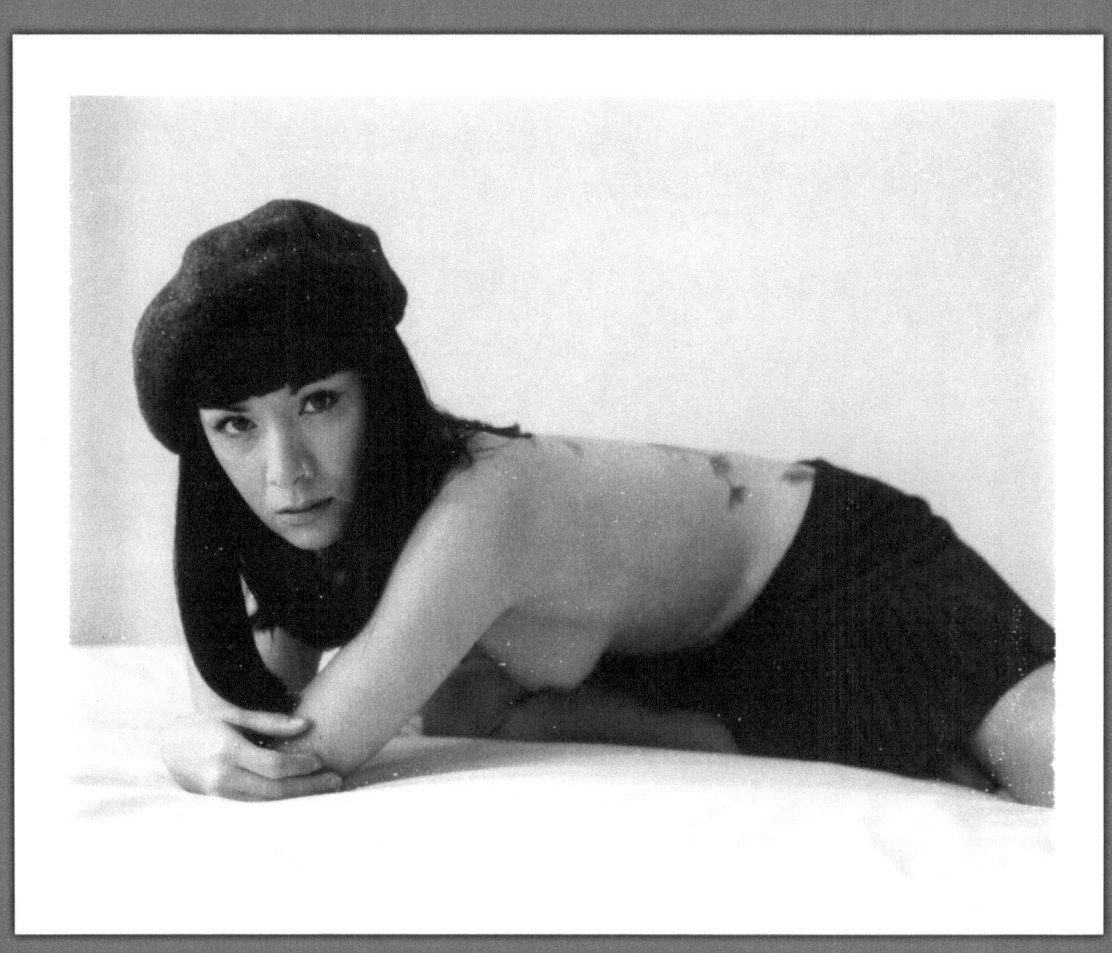

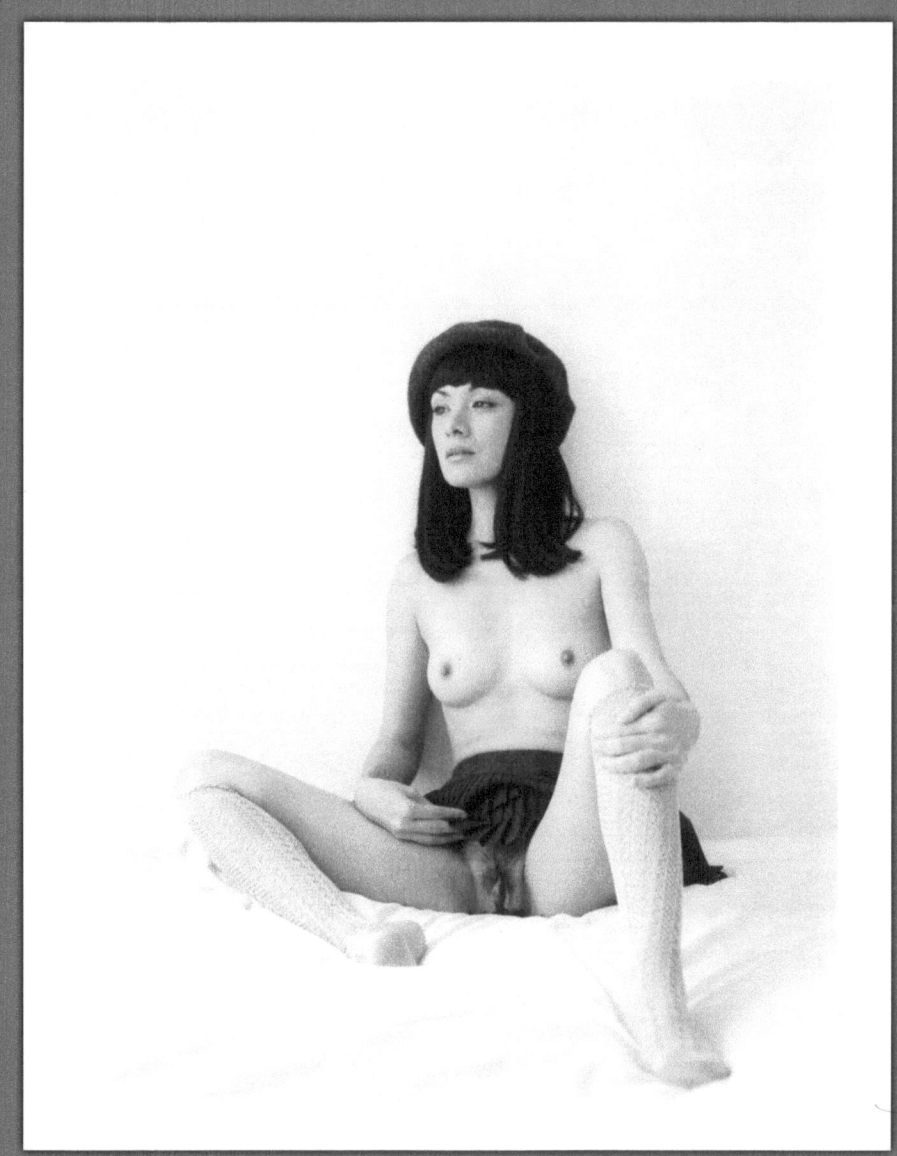

Kristen

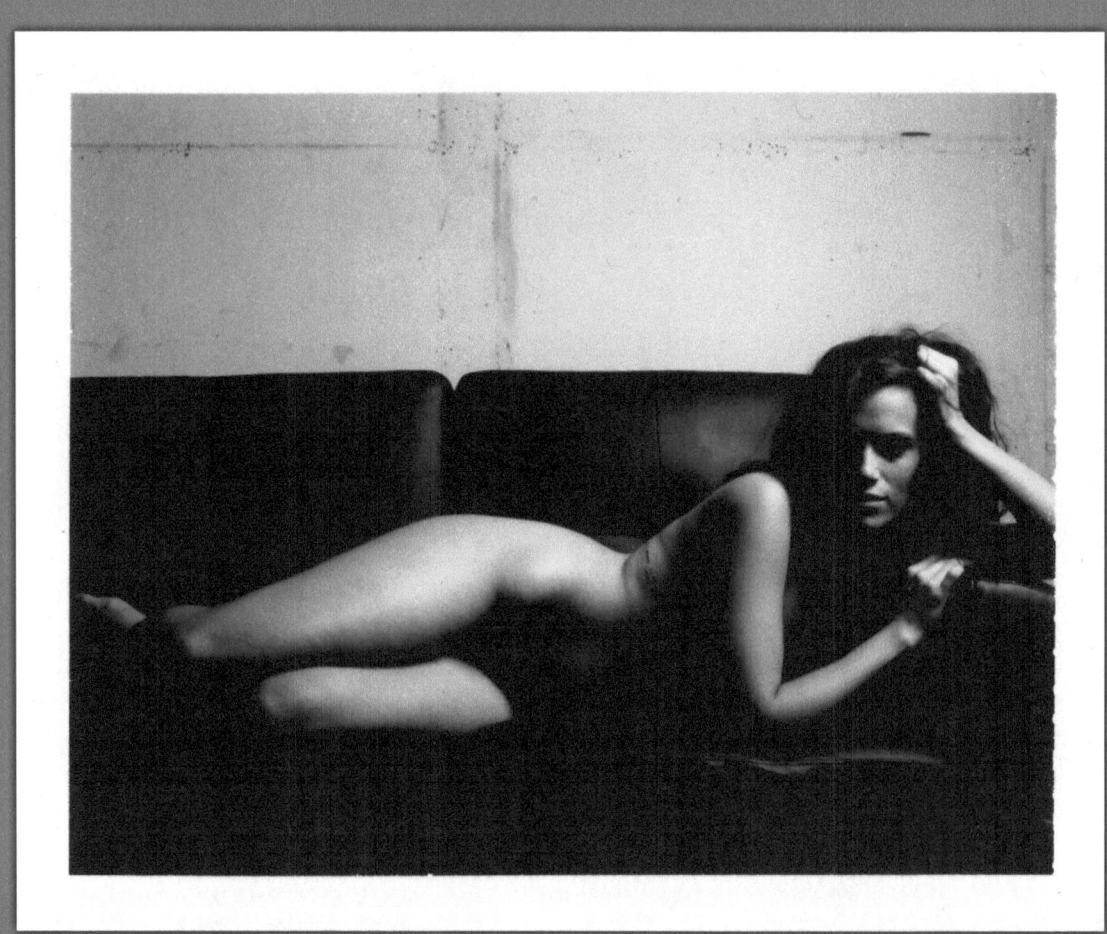

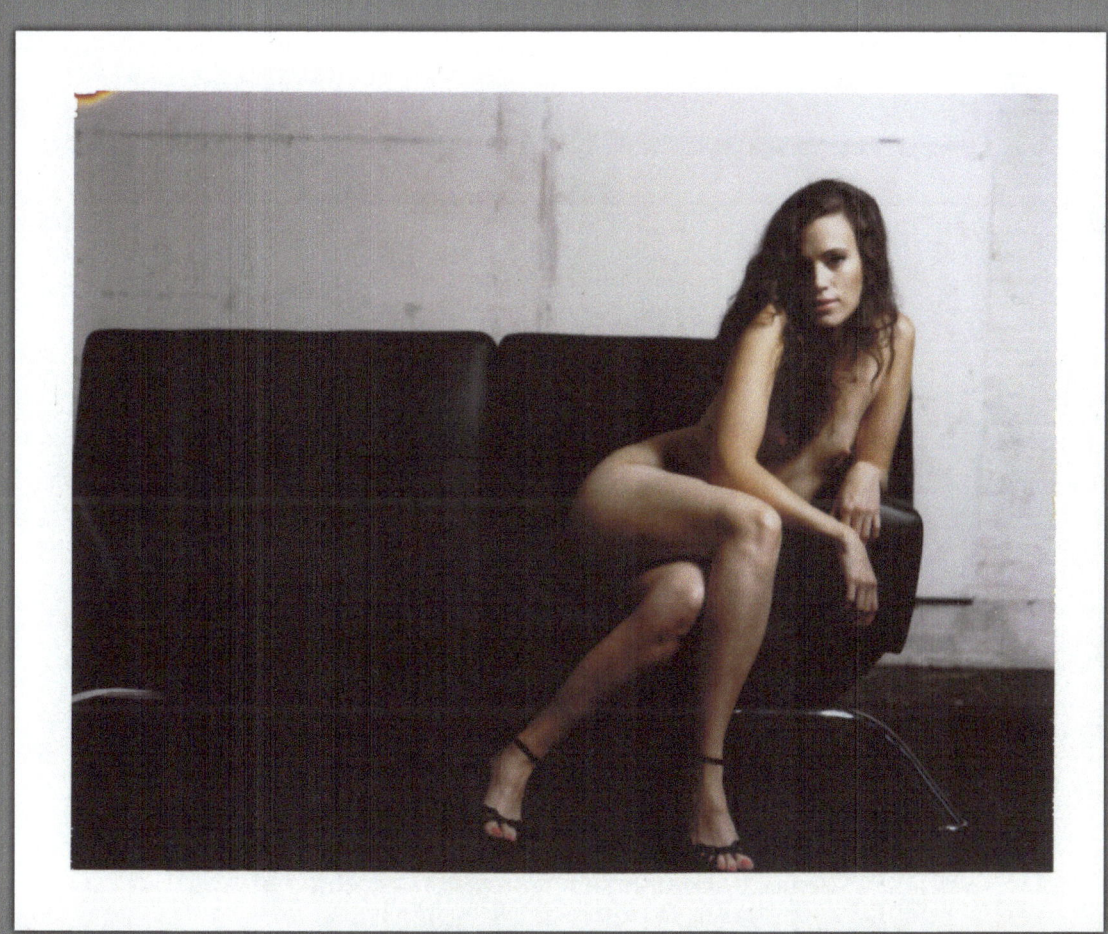

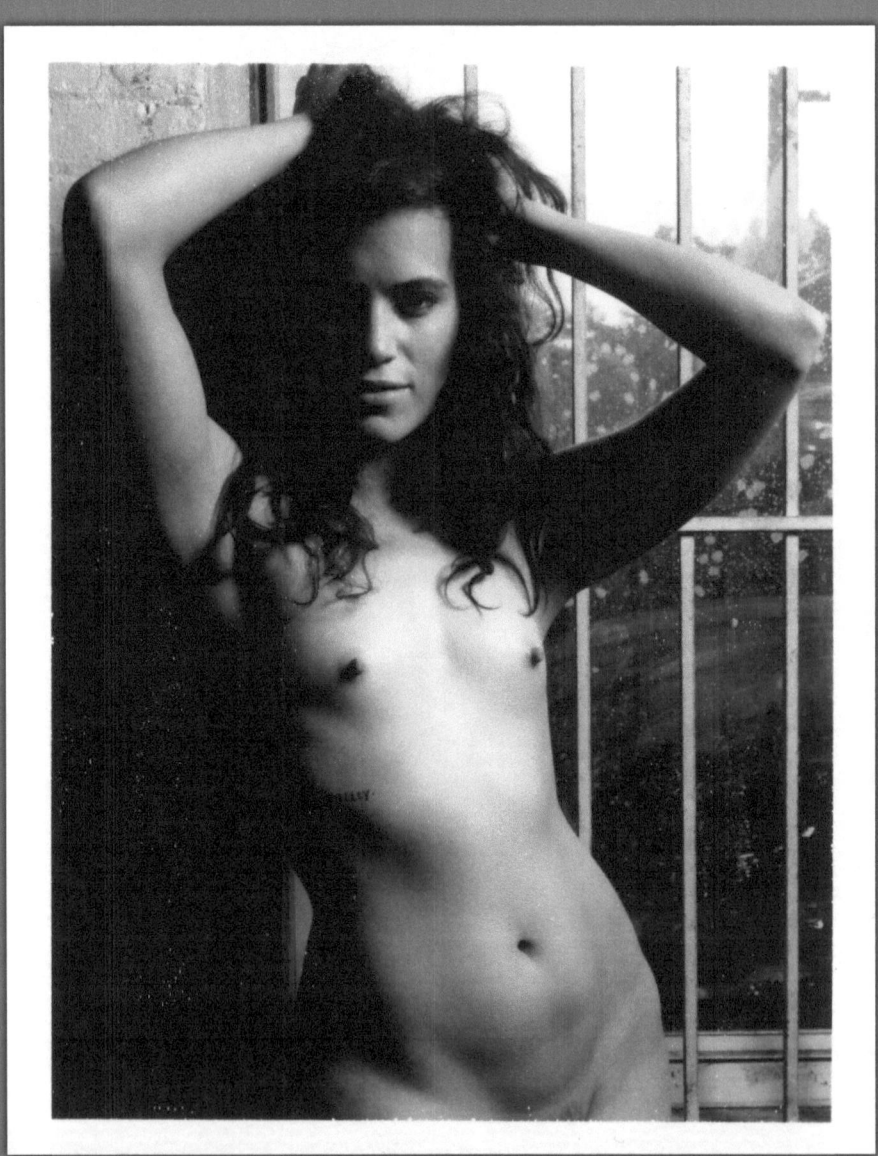

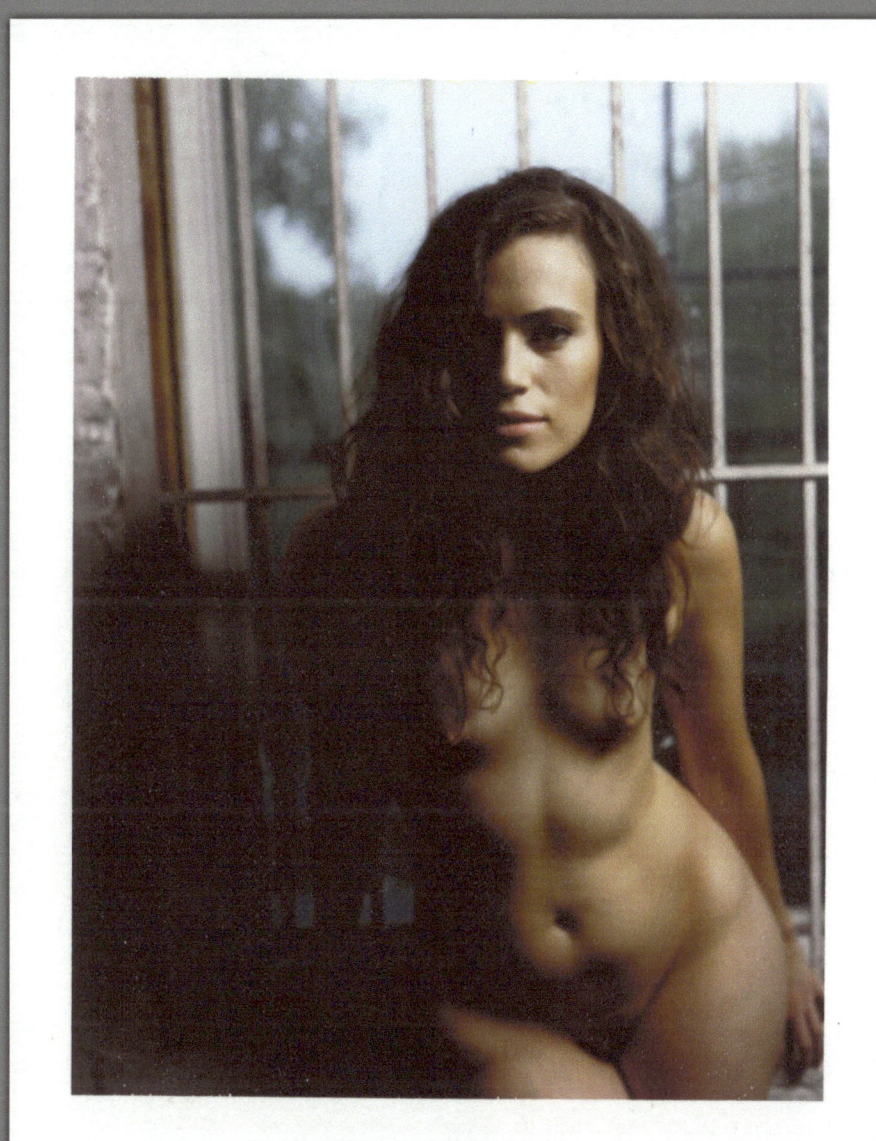

www.ingramcontent.com/pod-product-compliance
Lightning Source LLC
Chambersburg PA
CBHW050713180526
45159CB00003B/1017